Choose To
Win!

Love,

D.L.

10 *to* Win

Thoughts and Ideas to Keep
Your Spirits High, Your Soul at Peace
and Your Dreams Alive

Dale Smith Thomas

MISSISSIPPI QUEEN
PUBLISHING

Publishing Info:
Mississippi Queen Publishing
P.O. Box 2446
Brentwood, TN 37024

Cover Photo: Kristy Belcher
Cover and Interior Design: Bill Kersey, KerseyGraphics

Printed in the United States of America

Contents:

Author's Note

I'M GOING TO BE VERY HONEST AND TRANSPARENT WITH you: this isn't the book I originally planned to write. With a computer full of book ideas and works in progress, I can assure you this was not among them. However, sometimes the book you didn't plan to write, but are called to write, appears when you're paying close attention.

Several months back, I was talking with a friend and another entrepreneur about how we start our days. We agreed that when we start the day buried in emails, plowing through our 'to-do' lists, and stressing about the day's challenges it can feel very overwhelming. It was then I suggested, "What if we changed this routine? What about protecting the first 10 minutes of each day?" I thought about the idea of shielding our minds and souls before diving into emails, social media, or dragging yesterday's challenges into today. "Let's start the day with 10 minutes of positivity," I proposed, and call it '10 to Win.' That was the moment the concept for this book began to form.

My intention was to change the direction of the day by how we began the day. It hit me during that conversation that this is a universal experience if we don't guard those precious early moments. Once the momentum starts, it's hard to stop. What if we dedicated that short amount of time to quiet, peace, and setting a positive tone before the day takes over? It's so easy to start with the stress of yesterday but to empower today we have to pause and redirect. We have to be intentional.

I have had a morning practice of turning to the quiet for a long time. While I spend an hour on it daily, most people tell me they don't have that much time in the morning. That's when it dawned on me: it could start with just 10 minutes. I knew that redirecting even 10 minutes could be powerful and then I began to create more ideas based on the 10 to Win philosophy.

I've learned from experience that it's the small things in life that make a big difference. So, "10 to Win" is designed to be impactful in its simplicity. This book is easy to read, affordable (just $10), and simple to implement—if you choose to do so. But remember, just as it is easy to do, it's equally as easy not to do.

Throughout these pages, you'll discover not only why the "10 to Win" philosophy is a game-changer but also how to apply its principles to your own life. Whether you're looking to propel your career to new heights, cultivate personal growth and resilience, or embark on an entrepreneurial journey, this book equips you with the knowledge and strategies that can help to make your dreams a reality.

"10 to Win" isn't about luck or overnight success. It's about harnessing the power of intention, discipline, and strategic thinking. It's about understanding that success is a journey, and I hope this book will serve as your guide, offering a clear path forward in the middle of the noise and confusion of everyday life.

In the following sections, we'll explore the core principles that make up the "10 to Win" philosophy and how they can be applied in various aspects of your life. From setting clear goals to developing resilience, from learning to choose happiness daily to improving your relationships "10 to Win" provides you with a holistic framework to tackle the challenges that come your way and seize the opportunities that show up in your life.

It is these 10 to Win principles that have guided me through some difficult times in my life. In 2020 my career was totally sidelined due to Covid and I wasn't sure at 60 years old I was ready to start over. But, these principles reminded me that my calling was bigger than a momentary detour and so I worked through and applied every single principle I am sharing with you.

These life principles — they're like having tools in a toolbox, and you get to choose how you use them. Some are quick fixes, like a 10-second solution, while others require a bit more time, maybe 10 minutes a day. And some need repetition to really stick. But the most important thing? Getting started and staying committed to it.

I'm not here to ask you to squeeze more hours into your "in demand" day. Instead, my suggestion is to redirect some of that time. Those 10 minutes you spend scrolling through social media? Swap it for personal growth. Or trade in 10 minutes of TV time for a bit of self-investment. If you've got extra time, mix and match what works best for you.

I am sharing with you through the pages of this book the principles I strive to live by every day. I encourage you to really pay attention to two things, what connects with you and even what you resist. It's often in the challenges that the real magic happens.

Thank you for spending your time with me and joining me on this journey. I'm thrilled to share that I'm back on out on the road speaking. What seemed like the end was really just a pause and a fresh start. I stuck to these principles and didn't let doubt creep in. The real game-changers in life? They're non-negotiable; they're the ones you stick with no matter what. Thanks for being a part of this journey with me. Let's dive in and help you create your own "10 to Win."

With Love and Gratitude,

Dale

For a Personal Message from
Dale Scan the QR Code Below

Dedication

For Greyson : May this book be a keepsake for you, a reminder of our special bond and the countless dreams you have yet to chase. All My Love.

PART ONE

Self-Discovery and Attitude Adjustment

10 to Win - Begin with The End in Mind

10 to Win - Know Yourself

10 to Win - Alter Your Attitude

BEGIN WITH THE END IN MIND

"Almost all of the world-class athletes and other peak performers are visualizers. They see it; they feel it; they experience it before they actually do it. They begin with the end in mind."

—Stephen Covey

Begin With The End in Mind

Understanding the Concept: A Reflection

I love the phrase "begin with the end in mind" and I remember years ago when I heard it for the first time. I had to pause and really think about it. What does that look like when you begin with the end in mind? What are the things we do in our lives where we MUST begin with the end in mind? One of the things where we absolutely must begin with the end in mind is with air travel. When you decide to fly anywhere, for any reason, you have to begin with your destination. You don't just show up at the airport and say to the ticket agent, "Just give me a ticket, I don 't care where I'm going." I am pretty sure if you did they would call security for you. When you book an airline ticket, you know where you are going, when you are going and usually when you are going to return. If you are using the GPS in your car or on your phone for directions you put in your "destination". You know where you are going and from there you are given guidance on how to get there.

Life's Blueprint: Starting with a Plan

Think about building a house. What do you start with? Many times when I ask that question I hear, "a foundation" but that is not what you begin with, you start with a plan. You know exactly what the house is going to look like before the contractor every starts to build. You have a clear mental picture. You can "see it" before the building process ever starts.

How many of us really do that with our lives? Do we really look at where we want to go, what we want to achieve, and how we want to feel? Do we take as much time to truly plan our lives as we do a vacation, or do we just freely flow from day to day and wake up and wonder what has happened to our lives?

I am beginning with the end in mind as I write this book. What do I want your 'end result' to be after you have read and, hopefully, worked your way through this book? What do I want to feel when I have finished writing this book? I want to feel that I have given you my absolute best and shared truth with you that can help you. I want you to walk away with at least ONE idea that you will continually put into practice in your life. There are many ideas in this book, but I want you to at least grab one and put it into repetitive practice in your life. Repetition is the mother of all skill. That is a quote you will hear over and over again throughout this book. We learn everything by repetition, and if you will repeat the ideas that work for you, they will become part of your daily life. This is going to be a journey back to you, and I want you to have fun as you discover more about yourself. Yes, fun. I want you not just to read these words but to have fun with the learning. I have had fun writing this book, and it's an honor to know that you, wherever you are, are reading these words that have come straight from my heart and soul.

This writing experience has been different from creating my other books. This time around, I am juggling being a new grandmother and a writer. My writing time is shorter and is interspersed with the joyful responsibility of taking care of my new grandson several days a week. These moments with my grandson – the laughter, the little giggles, and those heart melting smiles – have brought something new to my writing. The moment I started writing the section about happiness, my immediate thought was Greyson. As I am writing now, I am watching him sleep on the monitor, never knowing how much time I will have. I look around, and my desk is a wreck with pieces of this manuscript everywhere. Life is different now, but so beautiful. I hope when you read this book, you can feel that mix of life's chaos and joy in my writing experience with you. It's like I'm sharing not just a message, but a piece of my life with you.

I suggest that you grab your 10 to Win journal or a notebook to begin this 10 to Win journey with me. I have also added blank note pages in the book for you to jot down your thoughts. Take notes, do the work. I once read that note takers are the money makers. I love that. I know there are many ways to take notes. You can use the voice recorder or note pad on your phone. For me, it's just not as effective as writing it down. Research is also showing us that writing something down has a bigger impact than if we type it in our phones. Why? Why a journal and not on your phone? Because writing opens up a different part of your brain and it also help you to remember. Research from Princeton University found that writing notes by hand improves your ability to remember things long-term. I have found personally that I remember more if I actually write it down. If you are not used to actually writing things down I think you will be surprised how it can impact you. I challenge you to try it. Writing helps me remember, so now I have given up on my digital calendar, and I have gone back to a written calendar. Writing also helps me process challenges and uncertainty. Writing it out helps me get my mind out of the way so that the truth that is trying to show itself to me can show up. I am truly surprised when I go back and read the things that have come through me to the page when I make the time to write it out. I will share more in the section on journaling.

It's your turn now. Here is your very first exercise that embraces beginning with the end in mind. Start right here with this book. Why are you here? Why did you pick this book up and decide to read it ? What are you hoping to change in your life or even in your day? I urge you to NOT skip over this. Just ask yourself those questions and listen to what you hear inside your soul and write it down. I truly believe when you KNOW what you want from this book then you will find it. Maybe it's just a simple idea to make your day better, maybe it's more than that. It doesn't matter just think about what you are looking for.

This book is about making changes that can improve your life both personally and professionally. These ideas are easy to do but they are just as easy NOT to do. Now that you have answered the questions about why you started this book, let's take the next step. If you and I were sitting down having a cup of coffee and I asked you a few questions I wonder if you could answer them. Here they are: 1.) What do you really want in your life? Tell me 10 things that you want. Don't censor them, write them down. What comes to mind instantly? It doesn't matter what they are, just write them down. If no one else was going to see them, what would you write down. Let me say this, unless YOU choose to share them with someone else, no one should see them. This is between you and you ONLY! 2.) What things would you like to change in your life? They can be big things or little things. It can be as simple as I want to be healthier or I want to follow a dream I have had buried in my soul since childhood. It could be that you want to spend more time with those you love. I believe that whatever you think about instantly, you need to explore it and write it down. I promise you that you are going to hear me say that over and over and over again. Write it down.

Several years ago I was so blessed to attend Performance Coaching University and got to spend time in a weekend workshop with the founders, Jairek and Amanda Robbins. It was truly one of the most empowering weekends of my life. Take the time and look up their work. In one of the exercises they had us do a deeper dive into our lives and helped us go deeper with our answers. They taught us that with each question that you ask yourself, follow up with this question, why do I want that and keep repeating that question 10 times? Each question brought us closer to what we were really looking for. Look at the questions above and try the go deeper process. I want you to look at our 2 questions. Let's start with what do I really want for my life. Let's say your first answer is I really want to live a more positive life? Here is the 10 step process. 1.) Why do I want to live a more positive life? Answer, because I think I would be happier. Question 2. Why do I want to be happier? Answer, because I think it would effect my work and my personal life. Question 3. Why do I want to effect my personal or work life? Answer, I think I would be more productive and a better partner, parent and friend. You get the idea.. keep asking until you are 10 levels deep and you will have your REAL answer. Do that 10 level deep question on anything that you are questioning or considering and see what you discover.

Set Your GPS

I want to go back to the GPS idea. We all use GPS on our phones probably even more than the GPS in your car. I don't think I have ever used the GPS in my car because I simply ask my phone to guide me. When you program your GPS it doesn't need you to tell it where you are if your location is turned on, it knows where you are. Deep down your soul knows exactly where you are. I want you to think about this, the GPS in your vehicle will not start working unless you put the car in drive. One other thing to consider is that you really don't know if GPS is really working until you arrive. I know many times I think, 'this doesn't feel right', but it usually is. Another thing to note about your GPS is that it stops when you do. It also stops if you get off course and it starts redirecting you. So many times I have laughed at my GPS going a little crazy with the redirection when I have simply stopped to get coffee and maybe a donut. I believe we all have this internal GPS. Think about your internal GPS as your inner guidance. It's God, Universe, your higher self, your intuition, -whatever you want to call it- but we all have it built in. We here so much now about AI, Artificial Intelligence, well this is your II, your Infinite Intelligence. We have this internal navigation that will guide us if we are paying attention. But, it needs a clear destination, it needs to know where we want it to go and it needs us to pay attention when we are off course. There are always signs when we are off course. It's our personal "rumble strip". Rumble strips on the side of the road are loud when your car hits them and they get your attention. They indicate that you are off course. They warn you that you are headed off the road. They are your warning sign to course correct. I think we all have our own built in rumble strips called our intuition. When something feels off we need to stop and pay attention, not ignore it. It's our indication to course correct.

What are you thinking?

As we begin with the end in mind in our lives, it requires us to mentally rehearse where we want to be, regardless of where we are. Mental rehearsal grows circuits in the brain as if the event has already happened. It's been proven that the brain can't tell the difference between something real and something vividly and repeatedly imagined. However, science has shown us that we have about 60,000 thoughts a day, and 90% are the same ones we had yesterday. Same thoughts lead to the same patterns. Think about what you talk about. Are you talking more about your past or your future? If we truly want to move our lives forward, we can't be more in love with our past than we are with our future. It is so easy to talk about what has happened in the past, but if that past is NOT what we want in our future then we have to redirect.

Everyone that knows me knows that I love football. I love everything about it, and recently, I saw an interview where NFL athletes were asked how important they thought the 'mental' part of the game was to the outcome of the games. The athletes interviewed said they believed that 70% or more of the game was due to their mental mindset. Yet, when they were asked how much time they dedicate to improving their mental mindset, they all said, very little. Many people will say they know that mindset is a critical piece to success, yet they spend little time developing it. What if we treated our minds like the high-performance machine that it is? What if we tracked everything we consumed with our minds? We tracked the conversations we had, the television shows we watched, the books or magazines we read. All of those are things you are feeding your soul. Are the things you are consuming making you stronger, more confident, more resilient, and overall improving your well-being? Are the conversations you are having empowering you or draining you? Are the things you are feeding your mind helping you achieve the things you just wrote down that you want for your life? If not, why are you choosing those things?"

Here's the truth: If you have limited beliefs, you will have limited results. What you see in your imagination, what you think of yourself and your dreams, will become your belief, and your beliefs direct your actions. Consider it determined imagination. Take 10 minutes and just imagine yourself in your wish fulfilled. What do you see? What do you feel? Who is with you on this journey? Years ago, when I was competing in a state beauty pageant, I practiced this principle over and over again. Long before the results were announced, I saw myself with the crown being placed on my head. It wasn't really about the crown, but the opportunity that having that title would give me. Each night, for months before I went to sleep, I saw myself walking on the stage, answering the onstage question with clarity and purpose. I saw the crown being placed on my head. When I arrived at the competition, I asked myself, 'If I had already won the title, how would I act? Would I feel nervous? No. Would I engage and have fun with all of the other contestants? Yes.' So, that is exactly what I did. It could have been very easy to 'imagine' another outcome because, in the prior two years, I had also competed and had not won. This wasn't a small competition. This was a competition with over 50 other beautiful and talented contestants. I had to train and discipline my mind to focus on the result I wanted, not the result that had happened in the other two years. When I competed, I felt calm, confident, and I had a blast. I was translating my vision into being, and when the crown did go on my head, it was as if I had been there many times before because, in my mind, I had been there. I began with the end in mind. That lesson has stuck with me as I have continued to pursue even bigger dreams in my life.

I could have easily fed my fears and focused in the other direction. I believe with everything in my soul that if I had done that, I would not have won that competition. My energy, my belief, and my attitude would not have allowed me to be my personal best. Our focus on what has gone wrong, what could go wrong, what is wrong, will always limit what is right. Fear and doubt are self-imposed, and if you can create fear and doubt, you can also destroy it.

We have choices to either act out of our circumstances or act out of a vision. A circumstance may be fixed or unchangeable, but our experiences are not. One shift in perception can change our entire experience. You can choose to either live in the world you are given or live in the world that you create. I continue to choose to live in the world I create. I could not win under the old story I used to tell myself. What story are you telling yourself? When you doubt, you disallow your desires to show up. Despair and doubt will never change a direction; only a decision will. Clarity and imagination produce results. Where is your imagination leading you?

Whoever it is you were born to be, whatever your soul was destined to accomplish, whatever things you were born to learn, whatever lives you are supposed to help change — it's time to get serious and get going. We have to be the ones to turn off confusion in our lives and turn on clarity. Stop looking at where you are, and focus on where you are going.

Create Your Day

Begin your day with the end in mind and tell yourself that throughout your day, you will look for 10 good things. Imagine yourself looking back on your day and identifying 10 good things. Try it at least for a week. Here is what will happen: Your brain acts on what it predicts, and so tomorrow, your brain will be scanning for the good things. You had an easy traffic day, the sun was shining, you got a call or text from a friend, etc. Look for the good in every day. Jot them down. I have been doing this, and now during the day, I catch myself thinking, 'This will be one of my 10 good things.' I keep a small notebook in my car at all times. If I hear something that inspires me, think of another blessing, think of someone I need to reach out to, I write it down.

Beginning with the end in mind is a powerful approach to achieving goals and living a fulfilled life. It involves visualizing the desired outcome of any endeavor before taking the first step. By doing so, you create a mental blueprint of your destination, guiding your actions and decisions towards that ultimate goal. I believe this idea not only provides direction but also serves as a source of motivation, keeping you focused and aligned with your objectives, ensuring that every step you take is a meaningful one towards your ultimate goal. Dare to dream, and create the remarkable life you want to live.

So here we are at the end of the first section and I encourage you to take 10 minutes and PAUSE and ask yourself what your take away was from this chapter and how you will apply it to your life. #10toWin

10 To Win Quotes:

1. "The reason most people never reach their goals is that they don't define them, learn about them or even seriously consider them as believable or achievable. Winners can tell you where they are going, what they plan to do along the way, and who will be sharing the adventure with them."
   — Denis Waitley

2. "Our plans miscarry because they have no aim. When a man does not know what harbor he is making for, no wind is the right wind." **— Seneca**

3. "I am not a product of my circumstances, I am a product of my decision."

4. "The will to win, the desire to succeed, the urge to reach your full potential … these are athe keys that will unlock the door to personal excellence."
   — Confucius

5. "Begin with the end in mind. Start with the end outcome and work backwards to make your dream possible." **— Wayne W. Dyer**

6. "I would visualize things coming to me. It would just make me feel better. Visualization works if you work hard. That's the thing. You can't just visualize and go eat a sandwich." — **Jim Carrey**

7. "Visualize this thing that you want. See it, feel it, believe in it. Make your mental blueprint, and begin to build." — **Robert Collier**

8. "Look at things not as they are but as they can be. Visualization adds value to everything. A bigger thinker always visualizes what can be done in the future. He isn't stuck with the present."
   — **David Schwarts**

9. "The clearer you are when visualizing your dreams, the brighter the spotlight will be to lead you on the right path." — **Gail Lynne Goodwin**

10. Formulate and stamp indelibly on your mind a mental picture of yourself as succeeding. Hold this picture tenaciously and never permit it to fade. Your mind will seek to develop this picture!"
    — **Dr. Norman Vincent Peal**

Notes

Notes

KNOW YOURSELF

"Self Confidence is a super power.
Once you start to believe in yourself,
magic starts happening."

10 TO WIN

Know Yourself

The Beginning of Self-Discovery

Do you truly know who you are? I mean, do you really grasp the foundation of your being? You might find this question absurd. After all, you may believe that you know yourself quite well. You can rattle off your name, your address, your occupation, your family details, and various personal facts. But if we were to dive deeper, could you confidently answer the profound questions of self-discovery? I believe the pursuit of genuine self-discovery is an act of bravery and courage. It's a journey that can lead us to the most extraordinary aspects of our lives, and I applaud you for embarking on it. I firmly believe that engaging in this voyage of self-discovery will propel you to triumph in every phase of your life.

Throughout our lives, most of us have been told who we are and who we are not. From expectations of society to personal beliefs, we've often been defined by external influences. This chapter encourages you to truly embark on the journey of self-discovery, shedding the layers of external definitions to reveal your authentic self. I can tell you from my own experience that this journey is not only courageous but ongoing. In our lives, external voices often drown out our inner truths. We've been shaped by the perceptions of others, and our genuine selves often become obscured in the blend of who we intuitively believe we are and who we've been instructed to be. These external influences can test our authenticity, challenging us to sync with the images others have painted of us.

However, if you're ready to embark on a courageous journey toward self-discovery, you're in the right place. I invite you to step forward and embrace the process of understanding and celebrating your true self. It's important to acknowledge that this journey is not a one-time event, but a lifelong commitment. As long as you continue to evolve and grow, you'll remain on this path of self-discovery. I am continually on this journey myself, and I can tell you that it's both thrilling and occasionally challenging.

I recently came across Oprah's remarkable book, "What I Know for Sure." In this area of self-discovery and reawakening, I can state with certainty that what I 'know for sure' is this: lessons about yourself that need to be learned will continuously manifest through different people and scenarios until you truly understand the essence of these teachings.The truth is, all the negative messages we accepted as our truth continue to get triggered throughout our lives. We must confront these internalized falsehoods and step into our new truth. By practicing reflection and "rewriting" our past experiences from a place of self-love and empowerment, we can change how these events affect us and reshape our narratives.

Even though I have done this work and continue to do this work, I occasionally face experiences and circumstances that challenge one of my core issues related to self-doubt. Throughout my childhood, this doubt was deeply ingrained in my life's fabric, falsely telling me that I am not valuable and that my thoughts and feelings held no significance. These beliefs birthed self-consciousness, insecurity, fear, extreme shyness, and an absence of personal boundaries. I used to think that everyone's opinion mattered except mine, and I simply had to accept whatever life dealt me. My voice felt insignificant. Today, I realize that, as a child, I didn't understand myself well enough to state my needs and desires. I felt like I shouldn't speak up for myself. However, the choices I made as a child do not have to dictate my choices as an adult. I CAN speak up and honor myself as an adult, and so can you.

Here is some insight from my journey. You see, even though I've come to understand certain truths, there are moments when those old habits, thoughts, and feelings sneak back in. It's like I sometimes catch myself slipping into those old beliefs, almost like replaying an old tape in my mind. I might start thinking that I have to just take whatever life throws at me, without any say in the matter. But here's the good news: now, I can spot these thoughts pretty quickly. They don't hold their power over me for long anymore. It's like learning to see the rain but not getting wet.

Through persistent effort, I've trained my mind, as discussed in Chapter One, to pay attention to my thoughts and actions. Whenever those old feelings of doubt and insecurity rear their heads, I remind myself that I am a different person now. I know who I am, and I can make different choices. People who know me today as a professional speaker, traveling and speaking on stages worldwide, find it difficult to believe that I was once painfully shy and could barely engage with others. The transformation happened when I began to truly know myself, and you can experience this too.

I genuinely believe that some of the damaging messages we've internalized as truths continue to resurface throughout our lives in various situations with different individuals. As I've mentioned, these lessons persist until we comprehend them fully. They provide us with opportunities to confront ourselves and embrace our newfound truths, distancing ourselves from the burdens of our past. It's our inner deceptions that divert us from our innate power. When old messages begin to cast shadows on us, we can stop them with a simple question: "Is this my truth now?"

I firmly believe that engaging in meditation, moments of stillness, or prayer, however you choose to characterize it, is beneficial for the process of self-discovery. During these quiet times, I've been given insights into pivotal events in my life where I failed to understand and accept myself, consequently failing to stand up for myself. I acted out of sacrificial love rather than self-love. I'm not suggesting that we shouldn't care for and love others, but when we completely abandon our truth and authentic selves, we do ourselves a disservice.

I recently came across a practice that completely transformed the way I see myself. It is a 10-minute exercise. I select an event from my past where I was not acting out of self-love, personal power, or my true self, and I rewrite it from the perspective of self-love. I pose these questions to myself: 1.) How would I have acted differently if I had been guided by self-love? 2.) What words would I have chosen? 3.) What actions would I have taken? I encourage you to grab a journal or a notepad right now and set a 10-minute timer. Begin by contemplating this question: "Which event(s) from my past do I want to rewrite where I did not stand in my personal power?" I believe if you will really listen, an answer will surface instantly.

Revisiting and Revising the Past

In my case, much of my lack of self-respect has manifested within relationships, both professional and personal. There have been countless instances where I relinquished my personal power and deviated from my authentic self. I've revisited these experiences and dedicated 10 minutes to rewriting each one from a fresh perspective. For me, I've relived these painful moments far too often, and by giving them attention I continued to give them power. I eventually recognized that when I revisit past experiences and relive the associated emotions, that pain isn't confined to the past; it's happening in the present. I've come to understand that I can "relieve" my past pain not by "reliving" it, but by "rewriting" it. I'm convinced that if we can genuinely release these experiences, we'll cease to relive them. When I rewrite them from an empowered standpoint (even if only on an emotional level), I can transform how they impact me, and you can do the same. I craft the conversations I would have had if I'd operated from a position of personal power. I outline the choices I would have made, guided by that personal power. I explore how it feels to even imagine this "rewrite," and, for me, it's been incredibly impactful.

This is a practice I've developed while writing this book. When an event from my past comes to mind, I spend at least 10 minutes documenting how it transpired, how I've been haunted by it, and then I dedicate another 10 minutes to rewriting it. This practice is still new to me, but each time I rewrite the old story, it changes how I feel about the experience. I realize by rewriting the narratives of my past I create a new feeling in the present. I urge you not to skip this exercise. Allocate 10 minutes to contemplate how you would rewrite a difficult, pivotal moment in your life. If you commit to this practice, I'd love to hear about your experiences. Let's rewrite our narratives and pave the way for a new future.

Become Unstoppable

We must claim ownership of our own stories and reclaim our lives, especially if we've drifted away from our true selves and our personal truths. And I believe that most of us have drifted at some point in our lives. So, let's embark on a deeper exploration of your identity!

Even if I've never met you, I can confidently say this about you: you are extraordinary, purposefully placed on this planet, and gifted with unique qualities that are exclusively yours. I want you to learn to trust yourself and that innate internal guidance you possess. Perhaps that inner voice has remained hushed for far too long, and it's high time you nurtured the ability to listen.

This section contains questions that may challenge you to your soul, but I sincerely hope you won't gloss over them.

Take the time, even if you need to dwell on them for several days, to embark on this self-discovery journey. I promise you, it will be the most valuable journey you'll ever undertake. When you genuinely know, accept, and celebrate your true self, no one on this planet can strip that from you. You become truly unstoppable when you invest in things that others cannot take away from you – characteristics like your mindset, your truth, your character, and your vision. These will form the bedrock of your inner strength when life presents its challenges.

Consider this question: What is your greatest quality? Are you disciplined, kind, generous, positive, loving? Take some time and really think about this. Complete these sentences:

'My   greatest   quality   is
_____.'

'The thing I love most about myself is _____
_____.'

'The one thing I would like to change about myself is
_____.'

I honestly don't think most people can answer these questions easily because they're not the things we usually spend time considering. However, I wonder if I asked you to list the things you dislike about yourself, would you be able to do so quickly? My guess is that you could!

Why is it that we can instantly identify our flaws but struggle to pinpoint our strengths? Leadership expert Margie Warrell put it succinctly: "We tend to overlearn from negative experiences, using them as evidence to cement the stories we tell ourselves that hurt our relationships, limit our ambitions, justify our excuses, and siphon the joy from our days."

I believe that if we want others to honor, respect, and appreciate us, we must first understand and appreciate ourselves. We must challenge the stories we've constructed about ourselves and confront our inner critic, which often dictates what we are not and what we cannot achieve. Let's think about this for a moment: Can you name the people who discourage you? Think about it. Would you put yourself on that list? Do you undermine and discourage yourself internally more than anyone else does? Let me be very clear: no one can discourage you, anger you, or upset you without YOUR permission. We must step up and assume 100% responsibility for ourselves. We must recognize and accept that, once we gain clarity about who we are, the opinions of others simply do not matter.

Quieting the Inner Critic

We spend an inordinate amount of our lives listening to others and their opinions about us. Yet, we know ourselves better than anyone else ever could. Despite this, we often crumble in the face of others' words, energy, and actions—people who have never lived a single moment of our lives. We despise rejection and the feeling of not being accepted, but sacrificing our truth for someone else's acceptance is a path to personal bankruptcy. I hope you ask yourself this question every day: 'Who should I listen to the most?' You already know the answer – YOURSELF.

Quieting your inner critic is a journey of transforming one's mindset, fostering self-love, and building resilience. Our inner critic often emanates from our inherent fear of failure, insecurities, and perceived inadequacies, acting as a constant hindrance to our progress and well-being. It is essential to tame this internal negative voice to maintain our mental health and achieve our full potential.

The first step is to acknowledge the existence of the inner critic and understand its impact on our thoughts and behavior. Recognizing when our inner critic is speaking allows us to differentiate between constructive self-reflection and destructive self-doubt. Next, it's crucial to reframe negative thoughts positively. Instead of succumbing to self-deprecating thoughts, try to view challenges as opportunities for growth and learning.

As I mentioned before, I believe mindfulness and meditation are potent tools in this journey. They enable us to observe our thoughts without judgment and to detach from them. Establishing a habit of daily reflection for at least 10 minutes can help in developing a balanced perspective and diminishing the impacts of the internal critic.

Before I learned these truths, if someone treated me as though I were insignificant, I internalized that belief and began to feel unimportant. It was profoundly liberating when I realized that no one could make me feel unimportant; it was my choice. The unvarnished truth is that we should be so steadfast in our self-awareness that NO ONE's opinion of us should ever shake our self-perception. We must advocate for ourselves when no one else will. We should never look through the eyes of others to glimpse our own worth. Sometimes, we must remind ourselves that when we seek validation from others, we might be looking into shattered mirrors, hoping to see a reflection of ourselves.

So, how can you truly get to know yourself without relying on the validation of others? You must have a crystal-clear mental image of who you believe you are and who you aspire to become. Too often, the thoughts and language we use to describe ourselves do not align with the individuals we want to be. We tend to judge ourselves unfairly. Judgment is like pouring sand into finely tuned gears. What happens when sand gets into the gears? The engine grinds to a halt. Judgment will paralyze you. It will keep you stuck, and often, self-judgment stems from comparison. Remember, comparison is the thief of joy. While you can look at others for inspiration and learning, comparing yourself is rarely a winning game.

I think these questions about 'knowing yourself' are hard for most people to answer, and they can't do it without really giving it some time. We can tell you about the best restaurants, our favorite vacation spot, our children, our jobs, and yet we struggle with knowing ourselves and telling you our best qualities.

So, I hope you will stop and give these questions all the time they need because YOU ARE WORTH IT!

Get to Know Yourself

Here are 10 introspective questions to help you get to know yourself better:

1. What do I wish people truly knew about me?
2. What is my biggest dream?
3. What is my biggest fear?
4. What am I most proud of in my life?
5. What would others be surprised to know about me?
6. What one thing would I change about my life if ANYTHING was possible?
7. What prevents me from doing that?
8. What am I most proud of?

9. What do I want to change about myself or my life?
10. What 10 things can I do to make that happen?"

   At the end of this section, I urge you to pause and reflect on your takeaways from this chapter and how you will apply them to your life. Give yourself 10 minutes. Remember, self-discovery is a continuous journey, one where knowing and accepting yourself is the ultimate victory. #10toWin

10 *to* Win Quotes

1. "If you are not in the arena getting your ass kicked on occasion, I am not interested in or open to your feedback. There are a million cheap seats in the world today filled with people who will never be brave with their own lives, but will spend every ounce of energy they have hurling advice and judgement at those of us trying to dare greatly. Their only contributions are criticism, cynicism, and fear-mongering. If you're criticizing from a place where you're not also putting yourself on the line, I'm not interested in your feedback." — **Brene' Brown**

2. "The moment you accept responsibility for everything in your life is the moment you gain the power to change everything in your life."

3. "You've just got to know yourself, and know what you're worth, and know where you're going, and know that you can always, always learn more." — **Zoë Bell**

4. "Be aware of yourself and know yourself. No matter how much you have learned and how much you know, if you don't know yourself, you don't know anything." — **Suzuki Shōsan**

5. "Step into the fire of self-discovery. This fire will not burn you. It will only burn what you are not." — **Mooji**

6. Never waste your time trying to explain who you are to people who are committed to misunderstanding you.

7. "When you know yourself you are empowered. When you accept yourself you are invincible."
   — **Tina Lifford**

8. "There will always be someone who can't see your worth. Don't let it be you." — **Mel Robbins**

9. Grow so remarkably that people have to get to know you all over again.

10. Things change when you get to know yourself and start loving yourself. When you respect your time and energy, your value goes up because you get to know your worth.

Notes

Notes

ALTER YOUR ATTITUDE

*"There is little difference in people,
but that little difference makes a big
difference. The little difference is attitude.
The big difference is whether
it is positive or negative."*
—W. Clement Stone

Alter Your Attitude

Positive Attitude is a Choice, Not an Emotion

I've always believed that one of the most potent tools we possess in any domain of life is our ability to choose our attitude. Our attitudes aren't dictated by someone else's opinions or life's happenstances. William James summed it up beautifully: "Our greatest weapon against stress is our ability to choose one thought over another."

One thing I know for certain is this, our attitude is wholly within our control; it's a conscious choice, not an emotion. Each day you can choose to have a positive attitude or a negative attitude, it's all up to you. Life can throw us some curveballs, and while we might not always like them, how we react is totally up to us. I wasn't a naturally happy child. When I think of kids who seem to be effortlessly joyful, my first thought always goes to Parker Greenwood. The spirited youngest child of two close friends of mine, Parker's zest for life is infectious. I remember asking Kim, after being around Parker's infectious happiness, "Has he always been this upbeat?" Kim just smiled and said he's always had that spark, even as a baby. Now I see that same kind of joy with my sweet grandson, Greyson. He is only 8 months old but he is pure sunshine. As I said, I wasn't naturally that way. For me, finding that kind of joy has been a bit of a climb. I wasn't born with that built-in sunshine. I started really learning that my energy and attitude were my choice in my teens, and honestly, I'm still learning to live it out every day.

The Science of Positivity

In this section, I will provide you with 10-minute ideas to refuel your attitude and change your perspective. You might wonder why this is crucial. Research has found that positivity, whether you term it happiness or optimism, boosts motivation, engagement, creativity, health, and resiliency. Many think a positive attitude is superficial, but recent studies show that optimism significantly improves various business outcomes. Focusing on the negatives narrows our perspective and hinders us from seeing the countless options we have.

Negative influences surround us daily. We need to actively seek, create, feed, and maintain our positive state of mind. If we're always focused on the negatives, it's like we're walking around with tunnel vision, oblivious to all the opportunities surrounding us. You don't have to search for the downers; they're there. But the good vibes, the positivity? That's something we've got to chase, nurture, and keep alive. Because if there's one thing I've learned, it's this: If we want a life brimming with health and happiness, the ball's in our court. A positive attitude isn't just a fleeting emotion. It's a strategic mindset that, surprisingly, significantly improves our daily outcomes, from business to personal. Whatever habits we keep feeding, they'll continue to grow.

I encourage you to take a moment and reflect on your life. Are you leaning more towards optimism or pessimism? Do you often talk about your desires or your problems? Do you enable solutions more than defining the problem? While it's essential to recognize problems, it's even more crucial to empower solutions. How do you intensify something? By giving it your attention and energy. What we focus on gets bigger. If you want to take the power away from something, stop nurturing it. Essentially, it's about mindfulness and decisions. We must step away from autopilot and be more deliberate in our thoughts, leading to more purposeful attitudes. So, what strategies can we adopt to adjust our mindset and energy daily? If you're genuinely committed to shifting from negativity to positivity, you need discipline, even if it's just 10 minutes a day.

The Daily Tune: Setting Our Frequency Right

Desiring a transformation in your life means recalibrating your inner frequency. Think of it this way: if your heart craves country music from the station at 98.7, you won't find them if you're tuned into 92.5—the sound of rap. It's all about aligning your dial to what you wish to receive. So, what energy do you resonate with every day? Where have you tuned your mindset? If you're consistently synced with negativity, how can you expect to experience the light and energy of positivity?

Taking the Leap: Do You Truly Want to Change?

Are you truly intent on altering your perspective? Reflect on that for a moment. I sincerely think you'd not be reading this if there weren't an innate desire within you seeking growth, optimism, and direction. Are you set on fostering a mindset that sees opportunity even in challenging circumstances? If you're nodding in agreement, then consider this your beginning.

The Decision to Change

Let's talk training. Pledge to yourself that every day, you'll dedicate AT LEAST 10 minutes to nourishing the optimistic side of your spirit. Whether it's during your drive, in the quiet of the morning, or right before sleep — consistency is key. Remember, repeated actions become habits. So, when you consistently set aside those 10 minutes to bolster your positivity, it becomes second nature. Nourish this mindset with the books you read, the content you tune into, and the conversations you engage in. Even the social media profiles you follow or the quick clips you view can be sources. There's a wealth of free content out there that can feed your mindset, but the responsibility is on YOU to seek and embrace it. Genuine transformation boils down to one thing: a decision. A simple preference for positivity isn't enough; you must actively decide to be better today than you were yesterday. We're our own agents of change. External pushes can only do so much; true change ignites from within. While it won't guarantee flawless days, it ensures self-awareness, recognizing when we deviate from our set path.

Attitude Assessment

I want you to assess your typical day-to-day attitude on a scale from 1 to 10. Be truly honest with yourself. What would your friends, family, or colleagues say about your perspective? Is your glass half full or half empty in their eyes? While we often hear the distinctions between the optimist's half-full glass and the pessimist's half-empty one, the reality is that the glass can always be refilled. You're neither an optimist nor a pessimist; you're a chooser. So, which path will you choose?

If you're determined to elevate your attitude, consider thinking about these questions:

1. Which books can reshape my perspective? Think of 3 titles that you sense might uplift you. Of course, this one can be among them. Need ideas? At the end of this book, I've shared some transformative books that have changed my life. Make a pledge to either read or delve into an audiobook. Start with a commitment to read at least 10 pages of a good book a day.

2. What can I listen to for guidance? I frequently tune into insightful YouTube sessions. Seek those that resonate with you and bookmark them for easy access.

3. Which mentors can light my path? Write down the name of at least one mentor you'd love to integrate into your growth journey.

4. Who around you embodies the positivity you are striving for? Recognize at least one inspiring individual in your life. Write down the name of that person that is that shining light of optimism. I also challenge you to send a text or a note to that person and thank them for being that bright light in your life.

Having a brighter outlook isn't about ignoring the real world; it's about seeing challenges from a different angle and seeking solutions. This practice is known as cognitive re-framing,

and there's now scientific evidence pointing to its health bene-
fits. Here's something worth noting: negative individuals often
indulge in three things. They play the blame game, blaming others
or circumstances, they rationalize their pessimistic mindset, and
consistently complain. Remember, complaining about things
like traffic or bad weather won't change them. Often, we dwell
on painful memories more than the joyful ones. If you catch
yourself dwelling on harmful thoughts, take a moment to shift
your focus to a positive aspect, no matter how minor. Stick with
this brighter perspective for at least 17 seconds. After all, optimism and pessimism can't coexist in the same moment. So, the
moment you sense negativity encroaching, consciously pivot
your mindset.

We can't constantly speak negativity and expect positive
results. Celebrate and revisit the moments that bring you
joy. Consider maintaining a "positivity journal" to reference
during tough times, because we all face those moments of
doubt. Simply looking at that list can instantly change your
focus and shift your perspective.

The Power of Choice and Responsibility

Habits, whether positive or negative, are formed by us. If we've
fostered habits that bring us down, we possess the power to
transform them into uplifting ones. Those who are inherently
optimistic understand the significance of taking full ownership

of their lives. Recognizing that genuine transformation emanates from within, they don't let external situations dictate their emotions. Instead, they choose their responses to those situations. They firmly believe in their power to either accept the world as it's presented or mold it to their vision. Complaining and feelings of hopelessness won't alter one's life trajectory; only decisive action can. To truly embrace happiness, one must actively seek and surround oneself with positivity.

To feel good, it's essential to gravitate towards uplifting thoughts. What's the most positive thought you can think at this moment? Don't skip over this. Pause and really think about that simple question. At this moment, what is the most positive thought you can focus on? We must all be guardians of our own hearts and spirits. Growing up in the deep south, I saw many homes with screen doors. Their purpose? To let in light and air, but to keep out pests and nuisances. Remember, it's up to you to erect that mental screen door, safeguarding your mind and soul. You decide what gets access. If you permit damaging memories from the past to re-enter, they don't just linger; they dominate the present. Even if they're from years ago, if you let them 'take a seat,' as we southerners put it, the past becomes your present.

Feelings, whether rooted in the past or stemming from recent events, have a way of asserting themselves in the present moment. Even if an event happened years ago, if you continually replay it in your mind, it becomes as fresh and raw as the day it happened. That pain from your past can so easily become today's agony.Why let the wounds of the past dictate today's narrative? Embrace practices of self-love, cherish yourself, speak kindly to your soul.

Remember, while it's essential to acknowledge our past, we shouldn't be shackled by it. There's a saying, "You can't sail to new horizons while anchoring to old shores." You can't be bound by your history and simultaneously chase your future. Make the decision. When you intentionally pursue your life's purpose, you'll naturally drift away from things that once held you back. It's a beautiful truth - you can't alter your past, but the future? That canvas is yours to paint.

Chasing your purpose also means you leave behind the weight of external judgments, past errors, and even those who don't share or support your vision. The circumstances might not transform instantly, but the pace at which you move, the momentum, can shift drastically. As you race towards your purpose, remember, it's possible to leave behind all that doesn't serve your journey.

Harnessing the Power of Momentum in Your Thoughts

Consider the concept of momentum. Imagine yourself atop a hill, pedaling a bicycle. Once you set off, the momentum steadily builds, propelling you forward. Similarly, your thoughts work in a similar way. If you begin with a negative, painful thought, it can trigger a chain reaction, leading to more negative thoughts, creating a powerful, albeit undesirable, mental momentum. For meaningful change to occur, you must alter this thought momentum.

Instead of attempting to control situations or conditions beyond your control, focus on the one thing you do have power over—your thoughts. I recall a profound insight from Steve Harvey about what he called 'turn back moments' These are moments when pursuing your dreams becomes incredibly challenging, to the point where quitting seems easier. Turning back feels like the right thing to do. During a turn back moment, you may contemplate giving up on your dreams and the personal transformations that are necessary to achieve those dreams. However, what sets a turn back moment apart is an unwavering resolve and determination to press on, even in the face of overwhelming difficulties. It's a pivotal moment where resilience and commitment prevail, propelling you forward on your journey despite the adversity. These moments often mark a significant turning point in your life and can lead to remarkable personal growth and success.

Turn Back Moments

No one gets a free pass on these turning points in life, you know? We've all been there. Like I mentioned earlier, back in

2020, I hit a major turn back moment when my business was basically wiped off the map. I had a choice to make: either give up and walk away from my life's calling and purpose, or change the story I was telling myself and learn how to handle those tough moments. I could have called it retirement, but I realized it was another turn back moment and I knew my work was not done.

Whenever those nagging doubts start to creep in, it's time to break the pattern of overthinking and rewrite our own story! You and I, we're always just one thought away from completely turning our lives around, from experiencing the most incredible moments, and building the strongest relationships. It's all about how our thoughts shape our beliefs, and in turn, our actions. One thing I've picked up from some pretty amazing teachers I've had along the way is this: a belief is really just a thought that you continue to think.

Win From Within

You know, I realized a long time ago that the real challenges in life often aren't about the tangible stuff we can see. It's those sneaky doubts that creep into our minds, the hurtful words from others that have way too much power over us, and that constant comparison game. The more we work on building confidence in ourselves and our path, the tougher it becomes for negativity and doubt to take over. You just have to make that commitment to win the battle in your mind, win the battle each day. It's the battle against fear, uncertainty, doubt, and frustration.

As I have already mentioned, I truly believe that many of our thoughts and beliefs about ourselves are shaped by what others think about us. We have to stop seeing ourselves through everyone else's eyes.

Just remember this: when you're absorbing other people's opinions, it's a bit like watching athletes on a field or a court, and the fans up in the seats are yelling instructions at them. You've seen it, right? Spectators passionately shouting advice to these "pro" athletes, as if they know better. But here's the kicker—notice how they're never giving directions when everything's going great. They are cheering in support.

Now, consider this: those athletes have mastered the art of tuning out the noise from voices that don't really matter. They've learned to focus on their game. And guess what? You've got to do the same. This, my friend, is YOUR Game of Life, and no one else's. So, let's turn down the volume on those grandstand opinions, even if they're coming from your own living room. Let's take a closer look at the difference between being just a spectator and actually being a pro. What do you think sets them apart?

Spectator or Professional

At first glance, the distinction between a spectator and a professional may seem straightforward. The spectator is the one comfortably seated in the stands or in their living room, offering opinions, suggestions, and critiques from a distance. They are often quick to vocalize what they believe should be done, fueled by the emotional rollercoaster of watching a game or a performance.

On the other hand, the professional is the individual down on the field, court, or stage. They're the ones in the thick of the action, where the outcome of their efforts directly impacts their life, career, or dreams. Professionals have invested time, energy, and unwavering commitment to reach the level they're at. They've honed their skills through practice, faced adversity head-on, and learned to navigate the turbulent waters of success and failure.

What sets these two roles apart is the depth of involvement and the weight of consequence. Spectators can freely voice their opinions, but the outcomes don't directly affect their livelihood or personal growth. For professionals, every move they make on that field, in their business or on a stage carries real consequences, influencing their life and shaping their future.

However, here's where the lines blur: in the game of life, we all wear both hats at various points. We take on the role of the professional when we're actively pursuing our goals and dreams, and we become spectators when we observe and offer insight to others on their journeys.

Handling the spectators in our lives, those well-meaning but often unsolicited voices of advice, criticism, and opinions, can be a delicate and necessary skill. Remember, while it's important to consider input from others, you are ultimately the captain of your own ship. Handling spectators is about finding a balance between being open to valuable insights and staying true to your path and vision for your life.

One of my favorite quotes about the critics and specters in life is by Berne' Brown. "If you're not in the arena also getting your ass kicked. I'm not interested in your feedback." Berne' Brown

As this section closes out I would like for you to think about some of your "turn back" moments. Give yourself the credit for moving forward when it would have been really easy not to move forward. Make that victory list.

You know, changing your attitude can be a bit like turning a ship around. It's not always quick or easy, but the direction it takes you can be so worth it. Think about those moments when you catch yourself feeling a bit negative or stuck. That's like standing at the helm of your own ship. With a small, deliberate turn - maybe it's finding something to be grateful for, or just taking a deep breath and smiling - you start to change course. Before you know it, you're heading towards brighter, more positive horizons. And the best part? You're in control the whole time.

So here we are at the end of this section and I encourage you to take 10 minutes and PAUSE and ask yourself what your take away was from this chapter and how you will apply it to your life. #10toWin

10 To Win Quotes:

1. "Your mind will always believe everything you tell it. Feed it faith. Feed it truth. Feed it with love. Feed it positivity."

2. "Your faith can move mountains and your doubt can create them."

3. "Hope is always available. Win the battle of the day. The battle of fear, uncertainty, doubt, frustration and the battle of pessimism."

4. "Check your mindset twice as often as you check your phone."

5. "Gratitude and attitude are not challenges, they are choices." — **Robert Braathe**

6. "A positive attitude is a person's passport to a better tomorrow." — **Jeff Keller**

7. "To be an overachiever you have to be an over-believer." — **Dabo Swinney**

8. "A positive attitude causes a chain reaction of positive thoughts, events and outcomes. It is a catalyst and it sparks extraordinary results." — **Wade Boggs**

9. "Our attitude towards life determines life's attitude towards us." — **John Mitchell**

10. "Virtually nothing on earth can stop a person with a positive attitude who has his goal clearly in sight."
    — Denis Waitley

Notes

Notes

PART TWO

Choosing Happiness and Embracing Change

10 to Win - Happiness Is A Choice

10 to Win - Look up, Get Up

10 to Win - Change the Channel

HAPPINESS IS A CHOICE

"Happiness is a choice, not a result. Nothing will make you happy until you choose to be happy. No person will make you happy unless you decide to be happy. Your happiness will not come to you. It can only come from you."

—Ralph Marston

Happiness Is A Choice

Your Decisions Determine Your Destiny

In this segment, we're diving into the topic of happiness. I'm here to help you figure out what truly brings you joy and how to bring more of it into your life.

Think about this statement for a moment: "Every day, I have the power to choose happiness." Trust me, as a child, I did not understand this concept, and it was years before I truly understood this truth. Back then, I never realized that I could control my own happiness. I titled this segment "Happiness is A Choice" because I've learned over the years that happiness is something we can actually choose. It took me quite a while to figure this out, so when I had my son, Nick, I wanted him to learn this truth very early. I was determined to teach him that happiness is a choice from a very young age. So, when he was around 2 years old, I started greeting him each morning by saying, "Good Morning, Nick, you can choose to be happy today."

I wasn't about to buy into the whole "terrible twos" concept. I know that words have power and my intention was to guide him toward the "terrific twos," whether he liked it or not. I wanted him to understand that happiness isn't something that's handed to you; it's something that comes from within.

Now, there were moments when he'd give me that adorable scrunched-up face and in his sweet baby voice, he'd protest, "I don't want to choose to be happy." And you know what? I'd just reassure him that it was okay, that the choice was his to make. It really struck me then how my beliefs were so different as a child. I had always believed that my circumstances were the guiding factors in my happiness. However, thanks to a great mentor and my willingness to learn, I discovered that it was my decisions, not my conditions, that determined whether I was happy or not.

As Nick grew older, this lesson on choosing happiness became a fundamental aspect of our family's outlook. I made sure he knew it's perfectly normal to have tough days and moments when you don't feel like choosing happiness, but that even in those times, you still have the power to find a little bit of joy within yourself. It's incredible how this simple idea transformed not only Nick's outlook on life but continued to transform my own. As my friend has said often about her son, he's been both my student and my teacher. I can say the exact same for Nick. I remember a specific situation when he was racing cars. He had worked so hard to get into this professional series and he and his grassroots team had built his car and went through so many challenges to race. I don't remember how far into the series we were when he had some mechanical issues that actually put his car in the wall and it was destroyed. It was truly heart breaking for us all. I remember sitting behind him later that day as he watched as a spectator, not a driver. One of his friends that had be on this journey with us was sitting beside him with his head in his hands; he was just as devastated as Nick. I heard Nick say, " Kovan, this is all part of racing. There is nothing we can do about this now but focus forward. We will start over and come back." I didn't say anything, and I don't know if Nick ever knew I heard that conversation. At that moment, he was my teacher. As his mother, my heart was breaking because of all his hard work to get there, only for it to be stopped. This was his dream, now in parts on the side of the track, yet he "chose" to look forward. It served as another reminder to me that, regardless of our circumstances, we hold the key to our own happiness. Before I learned these principles I thought that happiness was at the mercy of external circumstances, things beyond my control. It's a common belief that if we just have enough money, find the perfect relationship, or attain that ideal body weight, happiness will magically follow. But the reality is quite different. Happiness is a daily choice we make, no matter what life throws our way.

Embracing Happiness

As I look back, I can tell you exactly when that all changed for me. I was a very shy, very insecure, and I think I can also say, a very unhappy child. My mother has even confirmed to me that I did not wake up happy like little Greyson does. My energy was much more negative. As a child I started to take piano lessons. I am honestly not even exactly sure why. But, at about age 8 or so, I started lessons. We bounced around from teacher to teacher for several years before we landed with a young woman that would change my life. She was only 15, while I was 13, but highly recommended and affordable. Little did I know that this choice would teach me far more than piano; it laid the foundation for many of the lessons in this book and literally changed my life. This young woman had been in a tragic car accident that left her with physical scars a few years earlier. Yet, she was choosing happiness. When we arrived at her house way out in the country, she greeted me with an infectious smile and an unparalleled positive spirit. Yes she was still dealing with her lingering limp and facial scars but her joy for life radiated from her soul.

I was honestly confused. So I asked her how she managed to maintain such happiness with the injuries she continued to face. Her response has continued to resonate with me all these years, leaving a powerful mark. She said, "Dale, they told me I might not live, but I did. They told me I might never walk again, but I did. So, what's your problem?"

I will never forget that moment. She was unwaveringly focused on the positive aspects of her life, refusing to wallow in self-pity despite the challenges she continued to face. Meanwhile, I, with a clean bill of physical health, found myself unhappy with nearly everything. From that day forward, that remarkable young woman, through both her words and actions, began teaching me a valuable lesson: happiness is a choice. She had made the conscious decision to be happy, regardless of her circumstances. That faith and determination culminated in her becoming Miss America and going on to preach and teach and sing across the country. For me, it was a slow process, but I gradually began to realize that if I wanted to change my life, it all began with that same decision to embrace happiness.

I wish I could tell you that during those years, I immediately embraced that truth and put it to work in my life, but that wasn't the case. I had developed a pattern of thinking that had become a deeply ingrained habit. Gradually, I began to recognize this pattern and initiated a process of altering the daily choices I made. You will hear me say, over and over again throughout this book, that every single change in every aspect of our lives stems from one fundamental thing: a decision. A decision is not merely a preference; it represents a point of no return, a commitment with no room for retreat.

I think about my friend Cheryl, who, despite facing numerous challenges that could have undermined her happiness, remained steadfast in her commitment to not give herself an easy way out. Both you and I stand just one significant decision away from transforming our lives. Embarking on the path to happiness starts with making that decisive choice, and it begins with a deep understanding of oneself.

What makes you happy? Can you instantly identify the things that make you happy? Is it difficult or easy? While writing this, I challenged myself to pause and do precisely what I'm asking you to do. Let me start by sharing 10 things that bring me happiness, and perhaps they might inspire you too. Of course, these can change on a day-to-day basis.

So, here is my top 10: a steaming hot cup of coffee in a massive mug, preferably before the sun's even started to rise, surrounded by a stack of books, my journal, and our sweet rescue cats. I feel total happiness when I'm sharing my message with a crowd, and I see that 'aha' look on someone's face—knowing that an idea I have shared has sparked a change. Happiness also comes from the heart-melting giggles of my eight-month-old grandson when we lock eyes. Happiness is also those deep, meaningful conversations with people I cherish. Those of you that know me personally know the joy I have in scoring a killer pair of shoes on a discount rack. One of my happy places is sitting by the water, anywhere, at any time. I love the joy of cooking a big meal for our adult children and listening to them laughing and catching up around the table. Game days with my husband, whether we're at the stadium or glued to the TV, that's happiness too. I know my greatest source of happiness will always be the hugs and 'I love you's' shared with the people I care about. Those are my quick top ten.

Now it's your turn! I'm challenging you, and I know you saw it coming—write them down! If you can, do it right now. I get that happiness changes over time, with different phases of our lives. Happiness is fluid, my friend. So go on, it's your turn. Make it fun, keep it simple, and let your gut instincts guide you. Trust me, once you start jotting them down, you'll start noticing even more little pockets of joy in your life."

Write down 10 things that make you happy either in the note section or in your journal.

The Science of Happiness

Happiness is not some destination we're desperately searching for; it's found in the smallest joys of the moment. When you start thinking about the things that make you happy, it's like turning on a faucet – they just flow. I actually began writing this segment while sitting in my grandson's nursery as he peacefully slept. Now, I'm here by the water, feeling the breeze and watching the fish jump. Pure happiness.

Scientific studies now confirm the immense value of happiness and gratitude. It's referred to as the power of positive psychology. Prior to the late '90s, research primarily focused on the opposite – unhappiness and pain. But when the focus shifted to happiness, well-being, strengths, and flourishing, the results were astounding. I won't delve into all the positive effects of choosing happiness and optimism as a strategy, but those choices can transform our health, relationships, and worldview. It's simply a shift in mindset that allows us to change our perspective by paying attention to where our focus lies and consciously adjusting it.

Over the past two decades, research has consistently shown that the more we nurture gratitude, the happier we become. It has also revealed that by "practicing" gratitude, we enhance our relationship satisfaction and build resilience in the face of life's stressful events. In essence, gratitude redirects our focus toward what we "have" instead of what we lack.

If negativity seems to be the norm, choosing a gratitude practice can shift the energy from negative to positive. Any behavior pattern we repeat tends to take over. Just like athletes who tirelessly practice drills, we must engage in a daily happiness and gratitude routine to build this skill. It's about doing the work, transforming our habits and thinking patterns. As a child, I practiced doubt, fear, and insecurity, but it wasn't until I turned 13 that I began to understand and change these patterns. So, let's consider ourselves like those athletes, doing the "work" to make gratitude and happiness our second nature.

Instant Happiness Practice

So, you might be wondering what you can do right away when you're stuck in a bad mood and feeling down. Well, first, take a moment to be aware and pause. Then, pick a gratitude or happy memory and immerse yourself in it for at least 10 seconds. Extend it for another 10 seconds. Remember, energy flows where your focus goes. You can't hold onto an unhappy thought and a gratitude thought simultaneously—it's just not possible. If you start incorporating this happiness practice into your daily routine and make it a habit, I can promise you it will work wonders and transform your life.

I believe that one thing that truly affects our energy and happiness is the language we use every day. No, I don't mean the language you speak. Mine is Southern, and on any given day, I practically need an interpreter! What I'm getting at is the words you use day in and day out. These words frame your day and set its tone. They also shape how you perceive yourself, your life, and others.

So, what are your go-to words? What do you automatically say when someone asks how you're doing? Do you even think about them, or are they just habitual words you say without really thinking about it? How much of your language leans negative? I once read that we need 10 positive thoughts to counteract one negative thought. That's a 10 to 1 ratio! Imagine, each time a negative thought about yourself pops up, you pause and find 10 positive ones. It's been proven that our brains work based on predictions. If you consciously start seeking out 10 positive qualities about yourself and the people in your life—whether personally or professionally— your brain will make this a daily habit.

Think about the people who matter most to you, and jot down 10 things you admire about them or 10 things you're grateful for in relation to them. This small shift in language can make a huge difference in your outlook and overall happiness.

Reframe It

It might seem easier to focus on the positive qualities in others, but the truth is, it all starts with you! Some of the most impactful conversations you'll ever have are the ones you have with yourself. We're often our harshest critics.

What if, every time you caught yourself saying harmful and hurtful things to yourself, you paused and thought about 10 things you like about yourself? I'm not saying you shouldn't acknowledge areas in your life that need improvement; we all need to do that daily. I'm simply asking you to "re-frame it."

So, how can you do that? Instead of saying to yourself, "That was so stupid," try shifting that dialogue to a more positive choice like, "I could have made a better choice." The world can be tough enough without us tearing ourselves down, but it all starts with being mindful. Catch yourself when you start down that slippery slope of self-degradation. Ask yourself, "Is this really true? What's a more positive way to describe myself in this situation?"

According to the National Science Foundation, the average person has about 12,000 to 60,000 thoughts per day. Shockingly, 80% of those thoughts are negative, and a whopping 95% are repetitive. If we keep repeating those negative thoughts, we end up thinking negatively far more than we think positively.

Repetition is the Mother of All Skill

Remember, repetition is the key to mastering any skill. We learned everything we know through repetition—walking, riding a bike, driving a car, and everything else. However, most of us don't realize that we do the same thing with our thoughts and language. We repeat our thoughts so often that they become our beliefs. So, if you keep making a case for your limitations, that thought eventually becomes your belief. The moment you become aware of the negative thought you're using, pause for just 10 seconds and find a more empowering thought.

Do you truly realize that what you say about yourself is what can either threaten or empower your destiny? It's not so much about what someone else says about you; the real battle is with your own words and thoughts. Others may offer their opinions or criticisms, but it only truly harms you when you pick it up, repeat it, and start believing it. Here's the blunt truth: what someone else thinks of you is none of your business. There are two types of business in this world: your business and none of your business. Your business is to stand as the guardian at the door of your heart, soul, and mind, protecting and cherishing them just as you would for someone you deeply love.

Now, as you reflect on the language you use when talking about yourself and the things you say to yourself, ask yourself this one question: "Would I say this to someone I genuinely love and care about?" If the answer is no, then why on earth would you ever say it to yourself?

Doubt has the power to kill, but disappointment, well, it has the power to direct. Doubt can annihilate your dreams, your spirit, your ambition, and your beliefs. You know what makes anything in your life stronger? It's your attention. Attention is the fuel. When you give your doubts attention, you're essentially feeding them and helping them grow stronger. So, let's turn that doubt into something else—discontentment. Discontentment can be redirected, and it can serve as the secret door to transformative change in your life if you're willing to embrace growth.

Here are some fun and simple ways to instantly inject more happiness into your life:

Happiness Playlist

Create a happiness playlist on your favorite music platform. Begin with 10 songs that you know will lift your spirits and make you feel joyful. I have a collection of music that never fails to get me dancing and boost my mood. You will also read in a later section that I also have a Power Play list. I create different playlists when I want to feel differently. Some of the songs on my happiness playlist include 'Happy' by Pharrell, 'Can't Stop the Feeling!' by Justin Timberlake, and 'Shake It Off' by Taylor Swift. Get creative and have fun with your happiness playlist! If you have kids, get suggestions from them, and when they aren't choosing happiness, you can turn on the playlist.

Social Media Influence

Structure your social media accounts to follow content that brings you happiness or inspires you. I post something positive daily, follow me. Be mindful of what you're allowing into your soul. Personally, I follow accounts that feature babies laughing, motivational quotes and inspiration. There's something about a baby's pure, joyous laughter that instantly elevates my happiness. Plus, science has proven that laughter relaxes your body, reduces stress, and even enhances your immune system.

Sunday Night Gratitude

As I mentioned earlier, gratitude is closely linked to happiness. I understand that daily gratitude journaling might be too much to add to your life, so here's a suggestion: make it a Sunday night ritual. You can do it by yourself, but I encourage you to involve your family or a friend. Each Sunday night, jot down and share your gratitude list from the past week. Write down 10 things that you were grateful for during the week and speak them out loud to someone else. Encourage them to share their list with you as well. Let's collectively contribute to making this world a happier place, starting with all of us!

I want to share what happiness "feels like" to me. It's like snuggling up in a cozy blanket on a cool evening. It's all about noticing those small moments that bring a spark to your eyes or a lightness to your heart. Think about the laughter of someone you care about, the calm of an early morning, or the simple joy of sipping your favorite coffee. Happiness isn't always found in grand, life-changing events; more often, it's hidden in the simple, everyday moments. When we open our hearts to these little joys, our lives become a beautiful collection of precious moments. So, here's a promise I try to keep with myself, and I hope you'll join me: let's take the time to see and treasure these tiny sparks of joy. Because believe me, happiness is always there, subtly woven into our daily lives, just waiting for us to embrace it in all its gentle, wonderful splendor.

So here we are at the end of this section and I encourage you to take 10 minutes and PAUSE and ask yourself what your take away was from this chapter and how you will apply it to your life. #10toWin

10 to Win Quotes:

1. "The key to happiness is knowing you have the power to choose what to accept and what to let go." — **Dodinsky**

2. "Happiness is an inside job. Don't assign anyone else that much power over your life."— **Mandy Hale**

3. "If it makes you happy it doesn't have to make sense to others."

4. "Every morning you have a new opportunity to become a happier version of yourself."

5. If the only prayer you said was thank you, that would be enough." — **Meister Eckhart**

6. "Attitude is a choice. Happiness is a choice. Optimism is a choice. Kindness is a choice. Giving is a choice. Respect is a choice. Whatever choice you make makes you. Choose wisely." — **Roy T. Bennett,** *The Light in the Heart*

7. Become so filled with happiness that it heals every part of you.

8. "Do not look for happiness outside yourself. The awakened seek happiness inside." — **Peter Deunov**

9. "The foolish man seeks happiness in the distance, the wise grows it under his feet." **—James Oppenheim**

10. "Happiness is a choice, not a result. Nothing can make you happy, until you choose to be happy. No person will make you happy unless you decide to be happy. Your happiness will not come to you. It can only come from you."

Notes

Notes

LOOK UP, GET UP

"Our greatest glory is not in never falling, but in rising every time we fall."

—Confucius

Look Up, Get Up

Positivity Amidst Life's Challenges

Up to this point, we've been talking about embracing positivity and making choices that infuse our lives with it. But, the truth is – life's a journey with its fair share of bumps and twists. Sometimes, we're going to face challenges, feel a bit let down, or even find ourselves feeling a bit low. There might be moments where it seems hard to find the strength to stand back up, stay positive, and keep moving forward. But, borrowing the words of my friend, Les Brown, remember this truth: 'if you can look up, you can get up.' Granted, it might be a slow journey, step by tiny step, and perhaps it'll take a bit longer than expected, but trust me, you have the strength within you to rise back up.

In this chapter, I will share some insights that can be your guiding light when the days feel a bit darker, and it's tough to find positivity. I'm going to share with you some of the tougher chapters from my own life. As we walk through these stories together, my hope is that you'll discover some useful strategies that can help you navigate your own rough patches.

Here's an undeniable fact: We all face tough times. There will be moments of negativity, filled with disappointment and frustration. Sometimes, our goals might seem out of reach, or our efforts might miss the target. Relationships we believed unbreakable may crumble, and we might lose friends or family when we least expect it. Life can bring pain in various forms, including health challenges. It's a universal truth: nobody is immune. We will face setbacks and, at times, find it hard to stand back up. However, it's not just about falling; it's about rising again. When our personal truths, beliefs, and aspirations outweigh our letdowns, we cultivate resilience and continue to advance. By equipping our inner soul with the wisdom from previous chapters, and remembering that dark days are temporary, we can ask ourselves the right questions to navigate through life's storms.

Have you ever caught yourself asking yourself questions like, "Why is this happening to me?", "Why are they treating me this way?", or "Why did that have to occur?" In my journey, I've realized that dwelling on these 'whys' rarely leads to clarity or gives me answers. It tends to anchor me in a past that I can't alter, trapping me in a state of mind and energy that's beyond my control. I firmly believe in taking complete responsibility for ourselves, especially when it comes to our health. Sometimes, it's essential to be introspective and ask, "Why did I make that decision, and what can I do differently?" Yet, there are questions whose answers will remain elusive. Continuing to ask questions that have no answers is similar to spinning our wheels in the mud, making no progress.

Navigating Life's Storms

Some mysteries of life are beyond our understanding and simply don't have answers. For instance, last year, I faced a profound loss when Steven, one of my closest friends for over 30 years, passed away due to an unforeseen health issue at the age of 61. It's a part of human nature to seek answers, so naturally, I found myself questioning why he had to leave us so prematurely. Yet, as I grappled with this loss, I realized that some questions, like this one, remain unanswered, reminding me of the hard truth about life's unpredictable nature.

In 2020, life took a turn with the loss of my father, my father-in-law, and my business. My father passed away at 86 and my father-in-law at 96, both from old age, not Covid. Their passing was a profound loss, yet we found comfort in knowing they had lived rich, fulfilling lives. Reflecting on it, I realize I didn't question their departure as I did with Steven.

Even though I have learned not to search for answers in the unexplainable, the pandemic posed a new challenge. After more than 25 years in the speaking business, questioning 'why' became inevitable as it echoed my experiences with personal losses. I was on the brink of my most successful year, but then, all of a sudden, every speaking engagement was canceled. Let me tell you, 2020 was tough, marked by tears for lost loved ones and the sorrow of not being out there, encouraging people when I felt like they needed it most, as I had always done.

As days merged into weeks, then months, and even years, I started to doubt if I could start all over again. At 60, it felt like the business I had devoted myself to for over a quarter of a century was gone. But then, one quiet morning, I had this realization deep within: "Your business isn't lost, it's just on pause." Covid may have temporarily paused my career, yet it couldn't touch my true calling, which has always been my deepest motivation.

Everything happening was beyond my control, but my response? That was all me. I clung to the principles I've shared here, refusing to let disappointment spiral into defeat. Sure, I could've thrown in the towel, called it 'retirement', but my calling was too strong. I wouldn't let something out of my control dictate my life. So, I got up – mentally first, then physically, every day, to 'go to work', even with nowhere to physically go.

No one was booking speakers, but I could still create every day. It was hard, no doubt about it, but I refused to let it defeat me. I couldn't hit the road for speaking engagements, but I could still spread my message through social media, write, and work on new books. And you know what? Being grounded turned out to be a blessing. I got to spend precious time in Mississippi with my mom and be there for my daddy in his final days. If I had been tied up with contracts and on the road, I would've missed that. So, in the end, God and the universe had the best plan.

There are so many things we do NOT control, but here are 10 powerful things that we do control, and we need to keep them close when we are having experiences that are challenging to us. I urge you to write these down and come up with your own. When our lives feel out of control, we have to stop and remember what we can control:

You control when you get up and when you go to bed.

You control how hard you work on yourself.

You control what you listen to and what you read.

You control being on time.

You control if you study, practice, and grow.

You control your attitude and your gratitude.

You control if you keep your word or not.

You control if you speak kindly to yourself and others.

You control how you "view" a situation.

You control if you react or respond.

When we are facing tough times, times of loss, it's really easy to allow those feelings to take over. I recently heard Pastor T.D. Jakes say this, "God does not need anything you lost to bless you." Wow. That is so powerful. He also says we need to turn our wounds into wisdom. What if we looked at every wound and every disappointment as a stepping stone to greater wisdom? What if every difficult situation we viewed as a door to deeper growth? What if we asked ourselves this question; what 10 things can I learn right now from this situation, what wisdom can I gain?

Awareness, Acceptance and Action

I am mentioning in almost every chapter about the words we choose because I believe they are the keys to changing all of our behavior. When I lost my business, I could have said, "My business is broke. I have no money." But, instead I simply said, "Every day I am overcoming a cash flow problem." I stepped into these 3 things, awareness, acceptance, and action. The action I could take was changing my mind, and I could write and I could continue to share on social media. When we step out of the distraction of all the doubt and disappointment then the ideas will start to make their way to us. I knew that disappointment took me to the past where I had NO power.

I did not want to fuel that story. I started saying Covid did NOT take my business it is simply on hold and gave me time to be with my daddy.

Turning Loss Into Lessons

Here's the truth: you suffer when you think loss, less, and never. When we let go of something, even when it's a thought that is harming us, there is something deeper to be found if we look for it. Ideas and transformation can't make their way through frustration and depletion. You have to let it go. So much has been written about meditation in the past years. I don't remember hearing about meditation growing up. I know it's been a practice forever, but I also feel like we may have misconceptions about meditation. For me, it's simply getting quiet. It's no television, no social media. I have some guided meditations on my phone that help me quiet all the chatter in my mind. Our minds are on overdrive. Especially when we are facing challenges and we don't know where to turn, I have found meditation, quiet time, prayer time, whatever you want to call it, is the place where the answers begin to present themselves.

We all have internal guidance and again call it whatever feels right to you, but to hear that guidance you must get quite. I meditate and journal every day. It is my soul fuel, and my soul feels empty when I don't give it that space to refuel.

I am consistently amazed at the guidance and direction I receive in this space.

As long as we are stuck internally, we will be stuck externally. We have all heard that knowledge is power. No, knowledge is the beginning of understanding and taking steps into that understanding is power. Do not condemn the vehicle that brought you to where you are. Use it as a pivot point to move forward not as an anchor to your past. Whatever we push against we bring into our lives in a stronger way. When we feel stuck and things are not going how we hope they would go it's easy for the pain, the disappointment, the sadness, the fear, the anger and all of the other emotions to pull all of your attention. Remember that energy flows where attention goes. When you feel that negative drain pause, give yourself some time and let go of the thoughts for even a moment. Again, in the middle of pain find one gratitude. You can't hold both thoughts at the same time. When we let go of anything in our lives it's an opportunity to go deeper and find something inside you that needs to be found.

Tell A New Story

What conversations are you having around your pain or disappointment? I ask you to stop telling the stories that you do not want to repeat. Think about this, it doesn't matter when the event happened. It could have happened

10 years ago and you are still telling the story. The event happened 10 years ago but you are still experiencing the emotions now as if it just happened. I've heard people continuing to tell bad stories about their ex or their divorce and each time it's told those emotions come back and even get stronger. Stop dragging the pain of your past into your current life. It's up to you to start to lead yourself out of your discomfort. It's not up to anyone else. What is the story that you are telling yourself? If you are having a challenge and you need to "talk it out" call a trusted friend and tell them you need 10 minutes. Limit it to 10 minutes. You can tell the story, the problem in 10 minutes and then you ask your friend to help you talk through possible solutions. When we identify problems but empower solutions then we move our lives forward. Too many times we empower the emotion of the problem by giving it so much attention. Do you know how to take the power away from anything? You take your attention away from it. Think of it as a 10 to Win restart. You are not ignoring the situation that is bothering you. You are identifying it and then giving more focus to the solution. I encourage you to also use this principle with the people in your life. Use it with your children, your spouse, your friends, and your business associates. When they start telling you a problem, stop them and tell them you read an idea in a book that

you want to explore. Give them the 10-minute time limit to gripe, complain, tell all of the miserable details but at 10 minutes tell them time is UP. Then here are 5 questions you can ask them or yourself. There are also 5 affirmations to share with them or repeat to yourself. If you have no one to really "talk it out" with, then talk it out with yourself on paper. Write it. Be pissed. Be upset. Be whatever you need to be to get it outside of you. Release it but again, limit it to 10 minutes. I don't think you will need 10 minutes, but that is the limit. After you have released it here are the questions to ask someone else or ask yourself.

- What, if anything, can I do about this situation right now?
- What have I learned from this situation?
- Do I need to forgive myself or someone else?
- What one gratitude can I think of right now to change my energy?
- Every problem brings a solution. What one step can I take toward a solution to this problem?

Affirmations:

- I am wise, courageous, and strong, and I will be shown how to manage this situation.
- I believe in myself.
- I can do hard things.

- I am grateful for adversity because it helps me grow.
- Everything is unfolding in perfect timing. I release worry and choose to trust.

Start of Something New

When you are at a point in your life where you don't want to be, it's just a starting point for something new. We have to get over being disappointed, get over thinking it's not fair, get over feeling taken advantage of, getting over feeling overlooked. Every one of those things may be true, but it changes nothing. The only thing that can move you forward is you. When things are challenging and hard, it's easy to worry about everything. Worry is a waste of energy and time. It can't change the past. It can't control the future. It can only make today miserable. It steals your joy and takes away your ability to think about or see possibility. We don't grow when it's easy. We grow when it's hard.

I believe one way to start changing your mind and your mindset is to read or listen to "victory" stories. You can find stories of people who have overcome great odds on YouTube, Social Media, or just google. I encourage you to find 10 accounts that you can follow on Social Media that can inspire you. Find accounts on YouTube you can subscribe to that have information that will encourage you. I have videos on YouTube, and we are adding more. I follow many positive accounts on Instagram. If you follow me and need ideas, check out the accounts I am following that could inspire you. One other thing that always makes me laugh or lifts my energy when I am having a "character-building" day is the sound of babies laughing. There are so many great videos and reels of babies laughing. They are pure joy. They are pure positive energy.

Life is indeed a series of decisions – choices we make during the tough times and those we make when things are sailing smoothly. If you're reading this and you're in the midst of challenging times, I want to offer you a gentle reminder: You are here for a reason, a purpose that is uniquely yours. Every obstacle, every hurdle, is not just a barrier but an arrow pointing you towards the right path. It's in these difficult moments that our true direction often becomes clearer.

When faced with tough decisions, it's important to remember that these choices shape us, forge our character, and define our journey. They teach us resilience, wisdom, and the value of looking beyond the immediate. And in the times of success and ease, our decisions are equally important. They test our humility, gratitude, and the ability to stay grounded.

So, whatever you're facing right now, whether it's a mountain to climb or a smooth road ahead, embrace it as an integral part of your story. Each decision, each turn you take, is a step towards discovering more about yourself and fulfilling your purpose. Trust in your ability to navigate this journey, and see every challenge as an opportunity to grow and every success as a chance to reflect and be thankful. Remember, it's in the power of your decisions that your destiny takes shape.

So here we are at the end of this segment, and I encourage you to take 10 minutes and PAUSE and ask yourself what your takeaway was from this chapter and how you will apply it to your life. #10toWin

10 to Win Quotes

1. "Don't be a worrier. Be a warrior. Sometimes you have to be your own hero."

2. "Worrying does not take away tomorrow's troubles. It takes away today's peace."

3. "Sometimes we are tested. Not to show our weaknesses, but to discover our strengths."

4. "Challenges are gifts that force us to search for a new center of gravity. Don't fight them. Just find a new way to stand." — **Oprah**

5. "Your story of overcoming challenges will one day inspire others to survive."

6. "Believe in yourself and all that you are. Know that there is something inside you that is greater than any obstacle."

7. "When everything seems to be going against you, remember that the airplane takes off against the wind, not with it." — **Henry Ford**

8. "In the face of adversity, let resilience be your greatest weapon and perseverance your guiding light."

9. "Hardships often prepare ordinary people for an extraordinary destiny." — **C.S. Lewis**

10. "Adversities are temporary, what is permanent is what we become by the way we react to them."

Notes

Notes

CHANGE THE CHANNEL

"You can't start the next chapter of your life if you keep re-reading the last one."

—Michael McMillan

Change the Channel

Change Starts With Us

Many of us, while spending time with our families, have uttered the familiar phrase, "Please change the channel." This simple request lets our family know we would like something different, something more appealing or suitable to our current mood or interests. I think it's a straightforward yet profound analogy for the choices we face in life. You know, when you're watching TV and don't enjoy what's on, you simply reach for the remote and switch the channel, right? Well, it's kind of like that with our lives, too. If something's not working out or doesn't really line up with what we're aiming for, we've got to take action and switch things up. Just like changing channels on the TV, we need to be proactive in changing aspects of our lives that aren't fitting anymore.

I'm a big fan of the quote, "Life doesn't come with a remote, you have to get up and change it yourself." It's a real eye-opener because too many times, we find ourselves just waiting for things to change on their own. We wait for someone else to make the first move, for the economy to shift, or for a boss to give directions. But, you know what? The truth is, all change starts with us. It's in our hands.

I think one of the reasons I love this quote is because it is a powerful metaphor that encourages us to move away from passivity and embrace the act of taking charge. Just as we can't expect a TV show to change to our liking without us actively selecting a different channel, we can't anticipate that our life will shift in a more favorable direction without our direct involvement.

Choose Your Channel

Think of life as a television with countless channels, each representing different paths, choices, and opportunities. We often find ourselves stuck on a channel that no longer serves us, whether it's a job that doesn't fulfill us, a toxic relationship, or an unhealthy lifestyle. Yet, many of us remain passive, as if waiting for an external force to grab the remote and change the channel for us. But life's remote control is, in fact, in our own hands. It's up to us to make the decision to switch to a channel that aligns more closely with our values, dreams, and aspirations. The first step to any change in our lives is awareness. Just as we quickly identify a show that doesn't interest us, we need to develop the ability to recognize when certain aspects of our lives - be it our job, relationships, habits, or thoughts - are no longer contributing positively to our well-being.

Changing the channel requires effort and sometimes a leap of faith. It might mean stepping out of our comfort zone, confronting our fears, or making tough decisions. However, the act of changing channels is empowering. It's a declaration that we are not mere spectators in our own lives but active participants who have the power to choose our own narrative.

I have discovered this concept is not just about making big life changes; it's also about the small daily choices that shape our existence. Every decision we make, whether it's how we respond to challenges or the attitude we carry into our daily interactions, is like selecting a TV channel. By being mindful of these choices, we can ensure that the 'show' of our life plays out in a way that is more fulfilling and aligned with our personal goals.

In essence, the concept of changing the channel ourselves is a call to action. It's a reminder that we are the authors of our own story, and we have the power to change the plot at any moment. Life may not come with a remote, but it does offer us the freedom to choose our own path, to select the channels that bring us joy, growth, and fulfillment. It's a journey that requires courage, self-awareness, and a willingness to embrace change, but it's also a journey that promises a richer, more rewarding life.

In the introduction, I discussed how this book came to be, born from a conversation about the importance of the first minutes of our day. It's a universal experience to begin our day with minds filled with the remnants of yesterday's worries. Our thoughts race to our 'mental inbox'—leaping into emails, social media, or a cascade of concerns from the various challenges in our lives. While we allow our bodies and souls to rest and recharge at night, we often quickly revert to the previous day's issues without giving ourselves the chance to set a solid foundation for the new day.

In today's social media era, it's not uncommon for people to reach for their phones and dive into social media first thing in the morning. It's become a habit for many, and it often continues throughout the day, even before bedtime. But think about it: if social media is the very first thing you check upon waking up and the last thing you see before drifting off to sleep, perhaps it's time to reconsider this routine. Don't get me wrong; social media has its merits for connecting with others and gathering information, but is it replacing valuable personal growth time? Is it truly the foundation you want to build your day upon?

Be honest with yourself and ask: How much time are you truly dedicating to social media?

I believe that intentionally reclaiming those first 10 minutes in the morning and the last 10 minutes before bedtime can have a profound impact on your mindset and well-being. Instead of immediately checking social media, consider starting your day with a mindful practice or setting positive intentions. Similarly, in the evening, replace endless scrolling with activities that promote relaxation and restful sleep. Your overall quality of life may improve when you consciously choose how to begin and end your day, rather than letting social media dictate it.

I've read and discovered that spending just 30 minutes a day on personal growth equates to 28 eight-hour days of self-improvement over a year. Imagine the impact on your life! That 'soul fuel' would positively affect everything. However, I'm not asking for 30 minutes—not yet. This book is based on starting with just 10 minutes. Let's begin there, and perhaps you can gradually add more time. Use the first 10 minutes of your day to be mentally disciplined, to set the tone and foundation for what lies ahead. Set an alarm as a reminder that this time is your 10-minute 'refuel station' for the day. During these initial 10 minutes, leave yesterday behind and start afresh with a new vision, energy, and focus. So, how exactly do you do this? Here are some ideas to guide you. Choose what works for you and don't be afraid to switch things up. Find your own rhythm for the day and start with a higher energy level. Life presents enough challenges that can weigh us down throughout our days. If we begin already burdened by yesterday's troubles, it's tough to ascend from that point. Starting on a higher note not only empowers us, but it's also something we have complete control over. For years, we've been told that breakfast is the most important meal of the day because it lays the foundation. Think of this as your 'mindset breakfast' – the champions' foundation for a successful day.

Energizing Morning Playlist

I mentioned earlier the concept of a "happiness" playlist. I also suggest creating an "energizing" playlist. What songs can you add that will instantly boost your energy and positivity in the first 10 minutes of your day? What songs can you add that invigorate both your mind and body? Consider adding songs that are vibrant and dynamic, ones that make you feel alive and ready to take on the day. I know I am dating myself, but Earth, Wind and Fire is always on my energizing playlist. I have titled this playlist "Power Play" because all the songs on it are strong and powerful. Get your body, mind, and soul moving by creating your own energy-filled playlist.

Gratitude and Positive Affirmations:

Practice daily gratitude and positive affirmations. This can shift your mindset from a passive to an active stance. Write down three things you're grateful for every day and affirmations that reinforce your ability to effect change. If you can't make the time to write them down then record them on your phone. Make sure you record 3 new ones each day. At the end of the week go back and listen to them. You will hear the energy in your voice.

Mindfulness and Meditation:

Practice mindfulness and meditation to enhance self-awareness. I have leaned into this more in the past few years. I have found that this can help in recognizing when you're passively waiting for change and when you need to take action. There are numerous apps and online resources to guide you through this process. When I feel like I am "in demand" and have too much going on in my brain I choose a 10 minute guided meditation on letting go. I also have that playlist on Spotify for the days that I need to really slow down.

Those three suggestions are things that you can accomplish in 10 minutes. The last suggestion I am about to make has been life-changing for me for decades. While it can be done in 10 minutes, I personally require more time for it. If you find yourself pressed for time, consider setting aside a longer period once a week or once a month to try self-reflection journaling.

Self-Reflection Journaling:

I honestly don't know when I started this process, but I know for sure when it really clicked for me was after reading the incredible book by Julia Cameron, "The Artist's Way." It was recommended to me by a therapist during a period when I was facing some life challenges. At first, I was confused because I wasn't a writer at the time, and I wasn't sure how this could help me, but it was transformative. In "The Artist's Way," Julia Cameron introduces a practice known as Morning Pages, which quickly became a cornerstone of my creative philosophy. This exercise involves writing three pages of longhand, stream-of-consciousness writing, ideally done first thing in the morning. The purpose of Morning Pages isn't to create art or to write well, but rather to clear one's mind, sort through thoughts and feelings, and unearth creative energies and ideas that may be lurking beneath the surface. It's a form of mental decluttering that paves the way for clarity. Julia states that this practice helps in silencing the inner critic, overcoming creative blocks, and tapping into one's intuition and imagination. I can tell you that is exactly what it has done for me. By consistently engaging in this ritual, I found that I could cultivate a deeper connection with my inner self, leading to greater creativity and self-awareness. I discovered that this book was not just for artists but for anyone seeking a path to personal growth and creative liberation. If you are interested in this deeper dive I encourage you to get the book.

Journaling has been a time-honored practice with proven effects that span centuries. Its impact on mental health, creativity, and personal growth is well-documented and revered. Throughout history, journaling has served as a tool for self-reflection, allowing individuals to process thoughts and emotions, articulate goals, and preserve memories. Psychologists often recommend it as a therapeutic technique, citing its effectiveness in reducing stress, enhancing self-awareness, and improving mood. The act of writing helps to clarify thoughts, solve problems more efficiently, and can even boost the immune system according to some studies. Famous figures across various fields have relied on journaling to capture inspiration, work through complex ideas, and document their personal journeys, illustrating its enduring influence. Whether for historical documentation, emotional catharsis, or creative expression, journaling's longevity as a beneficial practice is a testament to its profound impact on the human experience.

I truly believe that just 10 minutes of journaling a day can be a powerful yet manageable step towards self-discovery and personal growth. This small commitment can strip away feeling overwhelmed with beginning a new habit and allows for a gentle immersion into the world of journaling. The practice, endorsed and followed by many influential figures, is not just about length but consistency and sincerity. For instance, Oprah Winfrey, a passionate proponent of journaling, has often shared how this practice has been instrumental in her journey towards self-improvement and success. Similarly, Ernest Hemingway, a literary giant, believed in the power of writing to clear the mind and inspire creativity. Mark Twain, another prolific writer, kept detailed journals throughout his life, which not only served as a reservoir of ideas but also as a personal sanctuary for thoughts and reflections.

Throughout history, journaling has been a favored tool among both renowned leaders and influential business minds. U.S. Presidents like Thomas Jefferson, Theodore Roosevelt, and Ronald Regan turned to their journals not just for recording daily events, but as a means of reflection and strategizing. Richard Branson, known for his entrepreneurial spirit, has often credited his success to the habit of jotting down ideas and reflections, which helps him stay organized and creative.

By dedicating just 10 minutes a day to writing in a journal, you align yourself with these great minds, using the power of written words to navigate life's complexities, celebrate successes, and process challenges.

One more note on journaling: I have started a journal for my 8-month-old grandson. I am writing to him and sharing things I want him to remember. I am sharing the lessons I wish I had known earlier. I want him to have something in writing from me that he can keep with him during his life journey. I wanted to share that because I thought it might inspire you to create a journal of thoughts and letters for someone else.

Step Out of Your Comfort Zone

I know that many of these practices require stepping out of your comfort zone. It's a bold act to defy the comfort of routine and the known, venturing into the realm of new experiences and challenges. This departure from comfort isn't just about taking risks; it's about personal growth and discovery. When you move beyond the boundaries of your comfort zone, you're presented with opportunities to learn, to stretch your capabilities, and to test your resilience. It's in these moments of uncertainty and discomfort that you often find your true strengths and untapped potentials. Embracing discomfort as a path to growth can lead to enhanced self-confidence, new skills, and a deeper understanding of yourself and the world around you. This journey, while sometimes daunting, is rich with the promise of transformation and empowerment, reminding us that the most significant growth often occurs in spaces that challenge us the most.

Adjust the Volume

One of the other thoughts about changing the channel is adjusting the volume once you decide the channel. Just as we adjust the volume on our TV, we must also learn to adjust the influence of external and internal voices in our lives. When we adjust the volume on our TV, we're essentially controlling how much impact the audio has on our viewing experience. Similarly, in life, once we've chosen our 'channel' or path, it's crucial to manage the intensity and influence of both external and internal voices. This involves consciously reducing the volume of negativity, whether it comes from the people around us, the media we consume, or our self-doubt and critical inner dialogue. It's about turning down the voices that drain our energy or discourage us and instead amplifying those that are positive, supportive, and uplifting. This can mean spending more time with people who inspire us, engaging with media that enriches our spirit, and practicing self-talk that is kind, encouraging, and empowering. Adjusting the volume also means being mindful of how we let the outside world affect our inner peace. It's about finding a balance where we stay informed and connected but not overwhelmed. This deliberate act of volume control allows us to maintain a healthier mental and emotional state, ensuring that our chosen life 'channel' is one that resonates with joy, growth, and positivity. This could mean reducing the noise of negativity and amplifying positive and supportive messages.

Change the Channel Challenge:

As we close out this segment I want to give you a change the channel challenge.

Start a 30-day challenge where each day, you make one small change in your routine or decision-making process. Embarking on a 30-day challenge to introduce small changes in your daily routine or decision-making process can be a transformative experience, fostering growth, resilience, and a renewed sense of curiosity about life. Each day presents an opportunity to step slightly out of your comfort zone and explore new possibilities, however small they may seem. Initiating a conversation with a stranger- maybe in a coffee shop, in the grocery store, or in a park, can open the door to fresh perspectives, interesting stories, and possibly even new friendships. Taking an alternative route to work or during your daily walk allows you to see different scenery, perhaps uncovering hidden gems in your own city that you never knew existed.

Beyond these examples, you could experiment with waking up 30 minutes earlier to indulge in the ideas I have shared above, switch up your exercise routine to challenge different muscle groups, give up social media for a few minutes of mindfulness or meditation. Even in decision-making, try opting for choices that aren't your usual go-tos. For example, if you're typically hesitant to voice your opinions in meetings, challenge yourself to contribute at least once per session. Or, if you usually avoid certain tasks, commit to tackling them head-on.

The beauty of this 30-day challenge lies in its simplicity and the compound effect of small changes. Over a month, these tiny shifts can lead to significant personal development and a deeper understanding of yourself. You'll likely find that what starts as a 30-day experiment may well evolve into long-term habits that enrich your life in ways you hadn't imagined.

Changing channels in your life can mean altering your mindset, focusing on gratitude, seeking new opportunities, or even changing the people you surround yourself with. It's about recognizing that you're not bound to a single narrative or path. You can always choose to tune into something that uplifts and inspires you. This shift might require effort and courage, but the control is always in your hands. Each channel change is a step towards a new perspective, a fresh start, and a path that aligns more closely with your aspirations and values. Embrace the power you have to flip through life's channels and find the ones that play the music of joy, growth, and fulfillment for you.

So here we are at the end of this segment, and I encourage you to take 10 minutes and PAUSE and ask yourself what your takeaway was from this chapter and how you will apply it to your life. #10toWin

10 To Win Quotes:

1. "Growth and comfort do not coexist." — **Ginni Rometty**

2. "The shell must break before the bird can fly." — **Alfred Tennyson**

3. "Everything you've ever wanted is one step outside your comfort zone." — **Anonymous**

4. "Life begins at the end of your comfort zone." — **Neale Donald Walsch**

5. "And the day came when the risk to remain tight in a bud was more painful than the risk it took to blossom." — **Anaïs Nin**

6. "Your life does not get better by chance, it gets better by change." — **Jim Rohn**

7. "If you want something you've never had, you must be willing to do something you've never done." — **Thomas Jefferson**

8. "A ship in harbor is safe, but that is not what ships are built for." — **John A. Shedd**

9. "If you are not willing to risk the unusual, you will have to settle for the ordinary." — **Jim Rohn**

10. "We can't become what we need to be by remaining what we are." — **Oprah Winfrey**

Notes

Notes

PART THREE

Building Relationships and Personal Empowerment

10 to Win - Relationships

10 to Win - Declaration and Affirmations

10 to Win - Acknowledgments and About the Author

RELATIONSHIPS

"I've learned that people will forget what you said, people will forget what you did, but people will never forget how you made them feel."

—Maya Angelou

Relationships

Everyone is Unique

This segement is probably the one that I love the most. If you know me personally, you're aware that I'm all about relationships. For those who don't, but are familiar with personality tests, I'm an Enneagram Type 2 and an ENFP in Myers-Briggs. I vividly recall taking these tests and feeling a sense of revelation. Going through the descriptions of my personality, each word struck a chord within me. Suddenly, the reasons behind my feelings of being different and not quite fitting in became clear. This was a pivotal moment in my journey towards accepting and celebrating my individuality.

It's a common saying that everyone is unique and possesses special gifts, yet sometimes, it can be challenging to truly believe in this. Back in part one we explored how to get to know yourself. I want to remind you that every person arrives on this planet endowed with a unique set of gifts, an exclusive blend of talents, abilities, and perspectives that distinguishes them from everyone else. These gifts are like seeds planted within us, possessing the potential to grow into something extraordinary. However, the journey to understanding and embracing these gifts is deeply personal and often challenging. It requires self-exploration, the courage to face both our strengths and vulnerabilities, and the willingness to nurture and develop our innate talents. This journey is not just about personal fulfillment; it's about contributing our unique piece to the vast mosaic of human experience. When we embrace our gifts, we not only enrich our own lives but also add value to the world around us, creating a tapestry of diverse skills and perspectives that can address the myriad of challenges and opportunities life presents. This process of discovery and acceptance empowers us to live authentically, aligning our actions with our true nature, and in doing so, we inspire others to embark on their own journey of self-discovery.

Foundation for Relationship Success

I took me years to learn this truth. The heart of thriving business and personal relationships truly blossoms from the loving and attentive relationship we nurture within ourselves. This self-relationship acts as a mirror, reflecting how we interact with others. When we nurture a healthy, respectful, and understanding relationship with ourselves, we are better equipped to extend these qualities in our interactions with others. Self-awareness is a critical component; it enables us to understand our own emotions, triggers, and boundaries, and it fosters more empathetic and effective communication with those around us. This inner harmony also instills confidence and authenticity, qualities that are magnetic in both personal and professional settings. When we are in harmony with our inner selves, it opens the door to heartfelt connections, fostering an environment rich in openness and honesty, and gently guiding us through the ebbs and flows of conflicts. By investing in our relationship with ourselves, we set a precedent for how we treat and are treated by others, paving the way for more meaningful, respectful, and fulfilling relationships in all spheres of life.

Here is a suggestion for you. Take some time and consider the 10 qualities you most desire in your valued relationships. Take a moment to genuinely think about it - do you really know what they are? Consider the characteristics you seek in a spouse or life partner, the characteristics that matter most in a best friend, and the traits you value in your business associates. Write these qualities down and study them closely. Now, turn the mirror towards yourself: do you embody and honor these qualities in your own life? For instance, if 'confidence' is on your list, ask yourself, do you practice and respect confidence within yourself? If not, why not? This introspection is not just about identifying what we seek in others, but also about recognizing and cultivating these qualities within ourselves. It's a journey of self-discovery and alignment, ensuring that we are not just seeking certain traits in others, but also nurturing them in our own character. This alignment between what we value in others and what we practice in ourselves is crucial for genuine and fulfilling relationships.

Life is a beautiful tapestry of connections, with some people woven into our lives for just a season, while others remain for a lifetime. Each person enters our journey for a reason, imparting lessons, memories, and experiences that shape us. It's important to recognize that not every relationship is meant to last forever. Some people are like chapters in a book, pivotal for the growth and development of the story, but not meant to stay till the end. The wisdom lies in understanding when someone's role in our life has reached its natural conclusion. Letting go can be challenging, but it's a necessary part of life's ebb and flow. Embrace the transient nature of some relationships with grace and gratitude, cherishing the moments shared and the growth they fostered. Remember, as some people exit, they make room for new individuals to enter, bringing fresh perspectives and opportunities for growth. Letting go is not a loss but a gentle release, allowing both you and them to continue your respective journeys enriched by the time spent together.

Bless With Love and Let Go

I've experienced both business and personal relationships that I was certain would last a lifetime, yet they came to an end. When my marriage with my first husband, who is also the father of my son, ended, I wasn't quite sure how to process it. Fortunately, I had immersed myself into learning, and many of these principles were deeply ingrained in my soul as our time together concluded after more than 15 years. Sure, either of us could have pointed fingers for the relationship's end, but playing the blame game never leads to success. As our time together drew to a close, I came across a phrase that began to resonate deeply within me every day: "I bless you with love, and I release you and let you go." Accepting that I would no longer share life with my son's father was tough. Trust me, it was even tougher for my mother. But I blessed our union with love, released it, and let it go. Now, decades later, I can say that this choice has been an incredible blessing. We remain friends and often are together with our spouses. I adore his wife, and he has been friends with my husband for a long time. We have a new grandson whom we all cherish, and it's truly a beautiful example of love, acceptance, and joy. I believe that my willingness to bless with love, release, and let go played a part in this. Of course, he had to be willing too, but I think my energy helped foster that. I wanted to provide the best example and environment for our son, he needed to see that even though we were no longer a couple, we were still united as parents. My husband and I, his two children and their spouses, my son, his wife and child, along with my ex-husband and his wife, all embrace each other as family. It may be unconventional, but our bond is wonderfully filled with love, joy, and acceptance.

I've continued to apply this mantra to business relationships and friendships that have reached their natural conclusion. It's not always easy, especially when a partnership genuinely enriched your life. However, clinging to something that isn't clinging to you isn't the way. If someone's assignment in your life has come to an end, be grateful for all it gave you. I encourage you to embrace this mantra: whether it's a relationship, a business partnership, or anything else that has moved on from your experience, bless it with love, release it, and let it go.

Imagine embracing this belief about all the relationships in your life: those who aren't in harmony with your spirit, your soul, your dreams, and your path, simply can't be there for you. What if we shifted our mindset, as I've discussed throughout this book, to celebrate the things and people who didn't show up, instead of wondering why they drifted away from us? How much more joyful and peaceful could our lives be?

Just today, my friend and creative director, Ashley, reminded me of this perspective. I was feeling upset about someone's behavior that seemed rude, and she pointed out, "They did you a favor. Your energies just didn't align." That was an eye-opener for me, instantly changing how I viewed the situation.

What if, every time we feel ignored, hurt, or taken advantage of, we gently remind ourselves that perhaps it just wasn't meant for us? This small shift in mindset can have a profound impact. Imagine telling yourself, "Those who aren't showing up for me are not meant to be part of my story right now."

Let's learn to celebrate and be thankful for the absences and the 'plot twists' in our story. Embracing this mindset can turn our life's narrative into one of gratitude and acceptance, enriching our journey with unexpected joys and serenity.

Power of Five

The wise Jim Rohn once said that we are the average of the five people we spend the most time with. Reflect on that for a moment. Imagine if you're consistently around people who are full of possibilities and positive thinking – don't you think their outlook would rub off on you? Conversely, if your time is mostly spent with individuals who are caught up in blame, excuses, and negativity, that's likely to influence you too, right?

Take a gentle look at your circle. While we can't always pick our colleagues, I'm referring to the people you choose to spend your time with. Do they bring growth and positivity into your life? Now, I'm once again going to ask you to "write it down". Write down the names of the five (or more) people you value most. We all encounter different kinds of people in our lives – I call them calculator people. There are those who add to us, multiply our joy, or perhaps, those who subtract or divide. Look at your list and place one of those symbols next to each name.

I warmly encourage you to invest more time and lend your ears more to those who add and multiply goodness in your life. Surrounding yourself with these people can create a beautiful ripple effect in your life, nurturing your growth and happiness. You may have heard of the "Let Them" concept from Mel Robbins. However, I found a poem that was written by Cassie Phillips that I wanted to share with all of you.

I believe that too many times we spend our time and energy wondering why other people make certain choices. Again, it's a question we may never have an answer for. I think this poem reminds us all to let people be who they are not who we want them to be. It's all about finding your own strength and having the guts to put your mental and emotional well-being first. It's not just about physically walking away from someone; it's more about giving yourself the space to breathe, to break free from all that negativity and any draining relationships.

It's really important for our own growth and happiness. We have to understand that we can't control what others do or how they feel, but we totally have the power when it comes to our reactions and who we let into our lives. Letting go, like the poem suggests, is really about taking care of ourselves, respecting ourselves. And you know what? It's a big step towards growing as a person and finding that peace and joy we all deserve in life.

Just Let Them

If they want to choose something over you,
    LET THEM.
If they want to go weeks without talking to you,
    LET THEM. If they are okay with never seeing
    you, LET THEM.
If they are okay with always putting themselves first,
    LET THEM.
If they are showing you who they are and not what
    you perceived them to be, LET THEM.
If they want to follow the crowd, LET THEM.

If they want to judge or misunderstand you,
    LET THEM.
If they act like they can live without you, LET THEM.
If they want to walk out of your life and leave, hold
    the door open, AND LET THEM.
Let them lose you. You were never theirs, because
    you were always your own. So let them.
Let them show you who they truly are, not tell you.
Let them prove how worthy they are of your time.
Let them earn your forgiveness.
Let them call you to talk about ordinary things.
Let them take you out on a Thursday.
Let them talk about anything and everything just
    because it's you they are talking to.
Let them have a safe place in you.
Let them see the heart in you that didn't harden.
Let them love you.
Author: Cassie Phillips

You know, the real job of our soul is to never ignore the lessons each relationship brings to us. It's like every person we meet, every bond we form, has something to teach us. And it's up to us to really sit with that, to mull over what we've learned and figure out our next move from that newfound wisdom. The thing is, we can't go around changing other people – that's just not how it works. It's all about focusing on ourselves, on our own growth and evolution.

In any relationship that really works, that truly thrives, it's about two people coming together, each fully committed to their own journey of self-improvement. But it's more than that. It's about being willing to be a part of something bigger, to be a supportive and positive force in each other's lives. It's like being teammates, you know? Each person brings their own strengths, their own lessons learned, and they're ready to share that, to blend it into this beautiful, cooperative dance of growth and understanding. It's not just about being together; it's about growing together, each person responsible for their own path but also ready to walk alongside the other.

Seen, Heard, Understood

As I wrap up this segment, I want to share something that's really close to my heart. I wholeheartedly believe that at the core of every truly meaningful relationship is this deep, almost instinctual need to be seen, heard, and understood. It's like everyone carries around this little internal universe, filled with thoughts, feelings, hopes, and fears. And what we really crave is someone who can look into that universe and truly see what's there. It's not just about acknowledging our presence; it's about recognizing our uniqueness, our individuality, the very essence of who we are.

Being heard is just as crucial. It's that feeling when someone not only listens to our words but also tunes into the emotions and intentions behind them. It's about feeling safe enough to express our innermost thoughts and knowing that they will be received with an open heart and mind. It's this amazing experience where our voice isn't just a sound in the room; it becomes a melody that someone else is eager to hear.

And then there's understanding. This might be the most profound need of all. It's one thing to be seen and heard, but to be understood is to feel truly connected. It's when someone grasps not just the what of your story, but the why. They get your joys and your struggles, your triumphs, and your fears. It's a two-way street, where empathy and compassion flow freely, and where judgments are left at the door.

In a relationship, fulfilling these needs creates a powerful bond. It's a bond built on mutual respect, deep connection, and emotional safety. When two people strive to see, hear, and understand each other, they lay the foundation for a relationship that is not just enduring but also enriching. It becomes a space where individuals can grow, not just side by side, but together, each person's growth nurtured by the other's understanding and support. It's the kind of bond where you're not just loved for who you are now, but for the many possibilities of who you might become.

I challenge you to pause and truly see, hear and understand the people that mean the most of you. It is the greatest gift you could ever give them.

Having positive, healthy relationships in our lives, whether they are friendships, romantic partnerships, family ties, or professional connections, is like nurturing a garden of varied, beautiful flowers. Each relationship requires its own kind of care and attention, but the fundamental elements are universal – respect, trust, communication, and understanding. In a healthy relationship, there's a harmonious balance where both parties feel heard, valued, and supported. It's about giving and receiving in equal measure, creating a space where vulnerability is met with empathy, differences are respected, and growth is encouraged. When we invest in fostering these qualities, our relationships become sources of joy, strength, and comfort. They turn into safe havens where we can be our true selves, share our deepest dreams, and weather life's storms together. Cultivating such relationships not only enriches our lives but also contributes to our overall well-being, reminding us of the beauty and strength found in connection and mutual care.

So here we are at the end of this segment, and I encourage you to take 10 minutes and PAUSE and ask yourself what your takeaway was from this chapter and how you will apply it to your life. #10toWin

10 to Win Quotes

1. "A great relationship is about two things. First, appreciating the similarities and second, respecting the differences."

2. "The most precious gift you can give someone is the gift of your time and attention."

3. "Learn to be quiet enough to hear the genuine in yourself, so that you can hear it in others."— **Marian Wright Edelman**

4. "Don't be upset when people reject you. Nice things are rejected all the time by people who can't afford them."

5. "Surround yourself with only people who are going to lift you higher." — **Oprah Winfrey**

6. "You will be too much for some people, those aren't your people".

7. "Become so confident in who you are that noone's behavior, opinion or rejection can affect you".

8. "It is not our purpose to become each other; it is to recognize each other, to learn to see the other and honor him for what he is." — **Hermann Hesse**

9. "Rejection is just re-direction". Bryant McGill

10. "Success in business and in life is all about connecting and building relationships." – Keith Ferrazzi

Notes

Notes

DECLARATIONS AND AFFIRMATIONS

"Affirmations are like planting seeds in the ground. It takes some time to go from a seed to a full-grown plant. And so it is with affirmations – it takes some time from the first declaration to the final demonstration. Be patient."

—Louise Hay

10 TO WIN

Declarations and Affirmations

Soul Fuel

As I bring this book to a close, I just want to say a heartfelt thanks for joining me on this journey. It's been a wonderful adventure, and I'm excited to leave you with something special – some declarations, proclamations, and affirmations.

I believe declarations, affirmations, and proclamations are vital tools for setting a positive tone and intention for the day. I consider them my soul fuel. Declarations are strong, definitive statements about one's goals or self, serving as a verbal commitment to a specific mindset or action. Affirmations, on the other hand, are positive, empowering phrases or sentences that one repeats to instill confidence and self-belief. They reinforce a positive self-image and mindset, essential for overcoming challenges. Proclamations, similar in nature, are public or announced statements, often used to share one's intentions or achievements with others, thereby creating a sense of accountability and community support.

Jim Carrey's story about writing himself a check is a fantastic example of how powerful affirmations can be. Before he hit it big in Hollywood, he wrote himself a check for ten million dollars for "acting services rendered" and dated it for the future. He carried that check around in his wallet, not just as a reminder, but as a declaration of his faith in his own dreams. It's like he was telling himself, "I'm going to make it, no doubt about it." This wasn't just wishful thinking; it was a bold affirmation of his goals and his belief in his ability to achieve them. His story really shows us how setting your intentions in such a tangible way can shape your mindset and drive your actions.

Every time he saw that check, it was a reminder of where he was determined to go. It goes to show, when we set our minds to something, really visualize it and put that energy out there, we start working towards making it happen. It's all about setting that intention, believing in our dreams and believing in ourselves.

Throughout this book, I have encouraged you to discover your true self, to silence the negative internal dialogue, harsh self-criticism, and the constant comparisons that can hold you back. It's a natural part of life to experience ups and downs in how we feel about ourselves, ranging from moments of great confidence to times when we feel like we can't achieve anything. It's important to acknowledge that encountering negativity is a normal aspect of life; it's all around us. However, as I've emphasized repeatedly, it's crucial to be deliberate in our pursuit of happiness, positivity, and in shaping the life we truly desire.

There will be days that are inherently more challenging, and it's on these days that having a personal declaration or set of affirmations on hand can be immensely beneficial. These can serve as powerful tools to inspire you from within, acting like a 'magic eraser' to wipe away those persistent negative thoughts that can start to play on a loop in our minds. Just like Jim Carrey's famous act of writing himself a 10 million dollar check as a symbol of his belief in his future success, your personal declarations are a testament to your self-belief and a commitment to your goals and dreams. They can be a source of strength and motivation, helping you to remain focused and positive, even on the toughest days.

This daily declaration that I have included below will only take just 10 minutes or so each day – morning and night. If you will take the time to write it out and customize it just for you, I know it will have even more power. But, this is a great place to begin. If you will stick with it, repeat it every day you'll start to see a shift, I promise. It's going to start reshaping your beliefs about yourself.

Like I said, if you will write it out and make it more personal then it will have even more power. For example under I am capable of achieving my dreams, define those dreams when you write it out. Be inspired by Jim Carrey and write yourself a check and look at it often.

10 to Win Daily Declaration

Today, I embrace the power of positive repetition and affirm my commitment to personal growth and success. I declare that:

I Am Capable: I am capable of achieving my dreams and overcoming any obstacle. Every challenge is an opportunity for growth.

I Choose Positivity: Today, I choose joy, positivity, and gratitude. I focus on the blessings in my life and let go of negativity.

I Am Worthy: I am worthy of love, respect, and success. My value is inherent and undeniable.

I Embrace Growth: Each day, I grow stronger, wiser, and more resilient. I learn from my experiences and use them to better myself.

I Trust Myself: I trust in my abilities and intuition. I am confident in my decisions and actions.

I Am Surrounded by Abundance: I recognize and appreciate the abundance in my life. I attract success, happiness, and prosperity.

I Am Confident: Each day, my confidence grows. I believe in myself and my capabilities.

I Cultivate Positive Relationships: I attract and nurture positive, supportive relationships. I am a source of kindness and encouragement to others.

I Control My Happiness: I am in charge of my emotions and today I choose happiness. My mood is a reflection of my thoughts, and I think positively.

I Am On My Path to Success: Success is a journey, and I am confidently walking my path, embracing each step with courage and enthusiasm.

I commit to these affirmations daily, knowing that through repetition, my actions and thoughts will align with my highest aspirations. This is my "10 to Win" declaration, a blueprint for a life of fulfillment, growth, and achievement.

Mental Soundtrack

I'm sure you've heard about the power of affirmations and positive self-talk, but have you ever wondered why it's so effective? The explanation, rooted in our brain's workings, is quite fascinating.

First, let's do a quick self-check. What's your daily mental soundtrack? Is it uplifting or does it drag you down? Take a moment to reflect on this and be brutally honest with yourself. Monitoring this internal chatter is crucial; it holds the power to transform your life, and you're the one in control.

Now, about writing down your affirmations: it needs to be done by hand. Yes, it's tempting to type them out quickly on your phone or computer, but there's something uniquely powerful about the act of writing. It clarifies your thoughts and solidifies those ideas in your memory. I also recommend reading your affirmations aloud, recording them, and playing them back regularly. This ensures the message seeps deep into your soul.

You've heard me say it before: repetition is key. It's a fundamental principle, not just for affirmations but for learning and skill development in general. The more we hear or do something, the more ingrained it becomes in our psyche. By consistently repeating positive affirmations, we start to believe them more deeply.

So, how does this work in our brains? Thanks to neuro-plasticity, our brain's ability to adapt and change, repeating positive affirmations can actually reshape our neural pathways. We weaken the old paths dominated by negativity and strengthen new, positive ones. This alters how our brain perceives and reacts to both internal and external stimuli, shifting our default state from negative to positive.

Affirmations do more than just make us feel good. They have a solid scientific backing. Neuroplasticity proves that our brains can change their structure and function based on our thoughts and experiences. Positive affirmations help form new, constructive neural connections.

There's also significant psychological research supporting this. For instance, the concept of self-efficacy, our belief in our ability to succeed, is greatly enhanced by affirmations. Studies have shown that affirming our values before a stressful task can even reduce our stress response.

Affirmations aren't just about positivity; they're about focus. They help us concentrate on what matters—our goals and values—and shield us from stress's negative effects. This focus improves our problem-solving skills and fosters a more optimistic outlook.

Consistent use of affirmations can also diminish negative, self-defeating thoughts. This aligns with the principles of Cognitive Behavioral Therapy (CBT), a well-established psychological treatment. By turning negative thoughts into positive ones, we effectively give ourselves a mental makeover.

And it's not just about the mind; affirmations can elevate your mood, boost self-esteem, and enhance self-efficacy.

In short, affirmations and positive declarations are more than optimistic mantras. They are tools for reshaping our brains, enhancing self-belief, focusing on our goals, reducing negative thoughts, and improving our overall mental health and mood.

Remember, repetition is foundational to our development and mastery of skills. It's through practice and persistence that we engrain the habits and mindsets needed for success. Whether it's forming habits, mastering skills, shifting mindsets, overcoming limiting beliefs, building resilience, or reinforcing commitment, repetition is the underlying force that drives progress and transformation. "10 to Win" harnesses the power of purposeful, strategic repetition, guiding you towards success and fulfillment.

Be Accountable

Let's explore the concept of accountability and the courage it takes to declare your goals to a trusted confidante. Embracing accountability is a deeply personal and enriching experience, and confiding your dreams with a friend or a trusted ally only adds to its significance. When you openly declare your ambitions to someone close, it's like weaving a thread of commitment that's stronger than just keeping these goals to yourself. It's about creating a bond over your goals and dreams, where their support and encouragement can be the gentle nudge you need on tougher days.

Imagine having someone who's not just a spectator, but a teammate in your journey. They're there to celebrate your little victories and offer a comforting word when things don't go as planned. It's this beautiful exchange of trust and encouragement that makes your goals feel more tangible, more attainable. There is a special kind of joy in sharing your progress with someone who genuinely cares. It's like having a personal cheerleader who's as invested in your dreams as you are.

By bringing someone else into your journey, you're not just seeking validation; you're embracing a partnership that magnifies your determination and commitment. This shared path of accountability isn't just about ticking off milestones; it's about growing and learning together, making the whole experience warmer and incredibly fulfilling. So, when you think about your goals, think about who you'd love to have by your side, cheering you on, every step of the way.

If you have that "someone" let them know about your journey through this book.Tell them about your dreams.

Read to them your declaration and make a proclamation to them and ask for their support.

The power of someone "holding space" for you during challenging times is immeasurable. It's about having that person who offers a safe, non-judgmental environment where you can be vulnerable, express your fears, and share your struggles without the fear of being criticized or advised. This compassionate presence provides a sense of security and comfort, allowing you to navigate through your emotions and thoughts at your own pace. When someone speaks life into you during these moments, they're not just offering words of encouragement; they're breathing hope and strength into your circumstances. Their affirmations and understanding help to lift the weight of your challenges, reminding you of your resilience and capability to overcome obstacles. This act of empathetic listening and positive reinforcement is a powerful catalyst for healing and growth, giving you the courage and confidence to face life's trials with a renewed sense of purpose and optimism.

You might think that, being so immersed in the world of personal development and positivity, I wouldn't need the same kind of support I encourage others to seek. But, honestly, I need it just as much, if not more. Pouring into others' lives takes a lot out of me, and it's those moments when I deeply appreciate the amazing people in my circle. They are the ones who catch me when I stumble, providing a safe space for me to regain my footing. They speak words of life into my days, gently nudging me back on track when I lose sight of my dreams. Remember, we all need someone who believes in us — that one voice that echoes our worth, especially in times of doubt. If you're feeling like you're missing that in your life, please reach out. I'm here to be that voice for you, to believe in you and support you, just as others have done for me.

As we reach the end of our "10 to Win" journey, remember, this isn't a conclusion but a new beginning. The principles and practices you've discovered here are the seeds of transformation, ready to bloom in your life. I challenge you, as you close this book, not to see it as the end of a chapter, but as the first step on your continuous path of personal growth. Carry these lessons with you, apply them daily, and witness the profound changes they bring. Embrace the journey with an open heart and a willing spirit. Remember, your growth, your success, your happiness – they're all in your hands. So, rise to the challenge, keep pushing your boundaries, and let your journey of self-discovery and empowerment continue. Your "10 to Win" is just beginning – make it extraordinary!

Here are 10 more powerful affirmations to help you cultivate a better life:

I Am Worthy of Success and Happiness: I deserve to be happy and successful. Every day, I move closer to my goals and dreams.

I Am Resilient and Strong: Challenges make me stronger. I have the resilience to overcome obstacles and thrive.

I Choose to Be Positive: I focus on the good in every situation. My positive attitude creates a life full of possibilities.

I Am Grateful for My Life: I appreciate the beauty and abundance in my life. Gratitude brings me joy and contentment.

I Am Constantly Growing and Evolving: Every experience is an opportunity for growth. I am committed to personal development and self-improvement.

I Am Loved and Valued: I am surrounded by love. I contribute positively to the lives of others and receive love and support in return.

I Am Healthy in Body and Mind: I prioritize my physical and mental well-being. A healthy body and a peaceful mind are the foundations of a good life.

I Am Confident in My Abilities: I trust my skills and intuition. I am capable and prepared to tackle any challenge.

I Create My Own Reality: My thoughts and actions shape my world. I have the power to create a fulfilling and meaningful life.

I Am Open to New Opportunities: Life is full of possibilities. I welcome new experiences that help me grow and bring joy to my life.

10 to Win Quotes

1. "It's the repetition of affirmations that leads to belief. And once that belief becomes a deep conviction, things begin to happen." — **Claude M. Bristol,**

2. "One comes to believe whatever one repeats to oneself sufficiently often, whether the statement be true or false. It comes to be dominating thought in one's mind." — **Robert Collier,**

3. "When I talk about doing affirmations, I mean consciously choosing words that will either help eliminate something from your life or help create something new in your life." — **Louise L. Hay,**

4. "Constant repetition carries conviction."
   Robert Collier

5. "You've go too win in your mind before you win in your life." — **John Addison**

6. "The ancestor of every action is a thought."
   — **Ralph Waldo Emerson**

7. "As a man thinketh in his heart, so is he."
   Proverbs 23:7

8. "The difference between success and mediocrity is all in the way you think." — **Dean Francis**

9. "Words can inspire. Words can destroy. Choose yours well." — **Robin Sharma**
10. "We need to change what we say and what we allow to be said in front of us." — **Brene' Brown**

Dale's Favorites

Here are a few of my favorite books and one of my favorite poems of all time, The Invitation. I hope you will find them as meaningful as I do.

Books:

What I Know For Sure - Oprah Winfrey

The Pivot Year - Brianna Wiest

The Artist Way - Julia Cameron

The Zero Point Agreement - Julie Tallard Johnson

The Book of Joy - Dalai Lama & Desomnd Tutu

The Age of Miracles - Marianne Williamson

Follow me on Instagram for Positive Quotes Daily: @ DaleSmithThomas

Sign up for Motivational Monday Magazine : www. DaleSmithThomas.com

Notes

Notes

The Invitation
by Oriah Mountain Dreamer

It doesn't interest me what you do for a living. I want to know what you ache for and if you dare to dream of meeting your heart's longing.

It doesn't interest me how old you are. I want to know if you will risk looking like a fool for love, for your dream, for the adventure of being alive.

It doesn't interest me what planets are squaring your moon. I want to know if you have touched the centre of your own sorrow, if you have been opened by life's betrayals or have become shrivelled and closed from fear of further pain.

I want to know if you can sit with pain, mine or your own, without moving to hide it, or fade it, or fix it.

I want to know if you can be with joy, mine or your own; if you can dance with wildness and let the ecstasy fill you to the tips of your fingers and toes without cautioning us to be careful, be realistic, remember the limitations of being human.

It doesn't interest me if the story you are telling me is true. I want to know if you can disappoint another to be true to yourself. If you can bear the accusation of betrayal and not betray your own soul. If you can be faithless and therefore trustworthy.

I want to know if you can see Beauty even when it is not pretty every day. And if you can source your own life from its presence.

I want to know if you can live with failure, yours and mine, and still stand at the edge of the lake and shout to the silver of the full moon, 'Yes.'

It doesn't interest me to know where you live or how much money you have. I want to know if you can get up after the night of grief and despair, weary and bruised to the bone and do what needs to be done to feed the children.

It doesn't interest me who you know or how you came to be here. I want to know if you will stand in the centre of the fire with me and not shrink back.

It doesn't interest me where or what or with whom you have studied. I want to know what sustains you from the inside when all else falls away.

I want to know if you can be alone with yourself and if you truly like the company you keep in the empty moments.

Acknowledgements

THIS BOOK, "10 TO WIN," IS THE CULMINATION OF A journey that would not have been possible without the unwavering support, belief, and hard work of some truly exceptional people. From the initial spark of an idea to the final product you now hold, this path has been one of immense growth and learning at every step.

I am deeply grateful to all those who believed in this concept and encouraged me to share this message. Your faith in me and this project has been a guiding light throughout this process.

A heartfelt thank you to my audiences around the world who continue to support my calling to share a message of empowerment. Your enthusiasm and engagement have been the fuel that drives my passion.

To my graphic designer, Bill Kersey, I extend a special thanks for your patience with my endless questions about "word count," and for your brilliance in crafting the book's cover and layout. Your talent and dedication have brought the essence of "10 to Win" to life in a visually stunning way. Thank you for being part of every book I have written.

My sincere appreciation goes to Clayton and Lambert Book House. Embarking on this maiden voyage with you has been an extraordinary experience, marked by collaboration and a shared vision.

And finally, to Ashley – without you, this book would not have seen the light of day. You have been my rock, standing with me, beside me, constantly encouraging me, and setting deadlines to keep me on track. On the days when I was filled with doubt, you found ways to rally around me and rekindle my motivation. Setting the release date was exactly the push I needed to move forward. Your unwavering support has been a cornerstone of this endeavor. I love you and am eternally grateful for your presence in my life.

To each and every one of you who has been part of this journey, thank you. This book is not just a reflection of my work, but a testament to the collective effort and spirit of everyone involved.

I am forever grateful.

Dale

About the Author

DALE SMITH THOMAS IS AN INTERNATIONALLY ACCLAIMED motivational speaker and best-selling author, renowned for her dynamic and inspiring messages that have captivated audiences worldwide. With a unique blend of humor, wisdom, and insight, Dale has become a sought-after voice in the realm of personal development and empowerment.

Her journey began with a deep-seated passion for helping others unlock their potential, leading her to a career that has spanned continents and touched the lives of thousands. Dale's engaging speaking style and profound understanding of human behavior have made her a beloved figure in the motivational speaking circuit.

In all of her books, Dale brings her wealth of experience and knowledge to the forefront, offering readers practical strategies for success and fulfillment. Her writings reflect her commitment to encouraging individuals to lead lives of purpose, positivity, and empowerment.

Dale Smith Thomas' unwavering dedication to inspiring change and fostering growth in others has established her as a leading figure in the field of motivation and personal development. Her latest book, "10 to Win," is yet another milestone in her mission to empower individuals to achieve their greatest potential.

For information on Dale Smith Thomas:
www.DaleSmithThomas.com or scan the QR Code

Other Books by Dale Smith Thomas
Solo In the Spotlight
Good Morning Gorgeous
Crown Up

Personal Message from Dale Scan this QR Code